Praise for
Raising an Emotionally Healthy Child When a Parent Is Sick

"Drs. Rauch and Muriel . . . provide sophisticated, developmentally appropriate advice, practical suggestions, and simple wisdom clearly and without jargon. I highly recommend their book."

> —Gerald P. Koocher, Ph.D.
> Professor and Dean, Simmons College,
> School for Health Studies
> President, American Psychological Association, 2006

"A must for any parent dealing with a serious illness. Its wisdom, insight, and commonsense advice are also invaluable to the spouse, partner, brother, sister, or friend supporting one who's facing the demands of raising children while struggling with illness."

> —Soledad O'Brien
> Anchor, CNN, "American Morning"

"This book helps you deal with the twin challenges of illness and raising children. Whether you are feeling confident or overwhelmed, Rauch and Muriel's logic and caring advice help you understand your child's perspective and respond in healthy ways. In doing so, you'll nurture everyone's hope and happiness in hard times."

> —Wendy S. Harpham, M.D., FACP
> Author of *When a Parent Has Cancer* and
> *Happiness in a Storm*

D1110336

RAISING AN
EMOTIONALLY
HEALTHY CHILD
WHEN A PARENT IS SICK

Also from McGraw-Hill and Harvard Medical School

Living Through Breast Cancer, by Carolyn M. Kaelin, M.D., M.P.H., with Francesca Coltrera

Eat, Play, and Be Healthy, by W. Allan Walker, M.D., with Courtney Humphries

Beating Diabetes, by David M. Nathan, M.D., and Linda M. Delahanty, M.S., R.D.

Lowering Your Cholesterol, by Mason W. Freeman, M.D., with Christine Junge

Healing Your Sinuses, by Ralph B. Metson, M.D., with Steven Mardon

Achieving Optimal Memory, by Aaron P. Nelson, Ph.D., with Susan Gilbert

Overcoming Thyroid Problems, by Jeffrey R. Garber, M.D., with Sandra Sardella White

The No Sweat Exercise Plan, by Harvey B. Simon, M.D.

Lowering Your Blood Pressure, by Aggie Casey, R.N., M.S., and Herbert Benson, M.D.

Healthy Eating During Pregnancy, by W. Allan Walker, M.D., with Courtney Humphries

RAISING AN
EMOTIONALLY
HEALTHY CHILD
WHEN A PARENT IS SICK

PAULA K. RAUCH, M.D.

AND

ANNA C. MURIEL, M.D., M.P.H.

McGraw·Hill

New York   Chicago   San Francisco   Lisbon   London   Madrid   Mexico City
Milan   New Delhi   San Juan   Seoul   Singapore   Sydney   Toronto

Library of Congress Cataloging-in-Publication Data

Rauch, Paula K.
    Raising an emotionally healthy child when a parent is sick / Paula K. Rauch, Anna C. Muriel.
       p.   cm.
    Includes bibliographical references and index.
    ISBN 0-07-144681-8
    1. Parent and child.   2. Child rearing.   3. Sick—Family relationships.
  4. Parents—Death—Psychological aspects.   I. Muriel, Anna C.   II. Title.

    BF723.P25R38   2006
    649'.1087—dc22

            2005027373

9 10   DOC/DOC   1 5 4 3 2

ISBN 0-07-144681-8

Interior design by Think Design Group, LLC
Interior artwork by Doron Ben-Ami

McGraw-Hill books are available at special quantity discounts to use as premiums and sales promotions, or for use in corporate training programs. For more information, please write to the Director of Special Sales, Professional Publishing, McGraw-Hill, Two Penn Plaza, New York, NY 10121-2298. Or contact your local bookstore.

The information contained in this book is intended to provide helpful and informative material on the subject addressed. It is not intended to serve as a replacement for professional medical advice. Any use of the information in this book is at the reader's discretion. The authors, publisher, and the President and Fellows of Harvard College specifically disclaim any and all liability arising directly or indirectly from the use or application of any information contained in this book. A health-care professional should be consulted regarding your specific situation.

This book is printed on acid-free paper.

This book is dedicated to
the devotion of loving parents
and the resiliency of children.

Contents

Preface

If you are reading this book, likely you or someone you love is living with a serious or chronic illness and you care deeply about the children who are affected. We are confident that children can grow up emotionally healthy, secure, and full of life when a parent is seriously ill. However, most parents can benefit from guidance on how to help their children to achieve this important outcome.

All parents learn about quality parenting from an array of different sources. They learn from friends, family members, teachers, pediatricians, books, TV, and their own experiences of being parented as a child. Most parenting information, however, assumes that parents are healthy. Parents living with a serious illness often feel their key questions and concerns are not being addressed. You will find this book filled with recommendations geared to help children of ill parents cope better. We hope reading this book will help you feel ready to face the special parenting challenges brought on by illness with new skills and renewed confidence.

It is common for an ill parent to look at other parents and to feel those parents have different priorities and fewer stresses to endure. Many describe times of feeling worlds apart from fellow parents. It is natural to feel resentful at times when healthy parents are complaining about how exhausted they are or alienated listening to a friend go on and on about how excruciating it is to wait for the results of a child's preschool admission or membership on a varsity sports team as if it is a life-or-death pronouncement. By comparison, ill parents and their partners may be wondering how to explain why they developed a particular medical condition or how to allay a child's fear about a parent dying.

Well-meaning family and friends often give inappropriate advice to ill parents about how to help their children. With the added burden of the illness, some parents lose confidence in their ability to assess what is right for their own children. They may be persuaded to override their own good judgment. We often hear examples of grandparents who encourage the parent to keep the diagnosis a secret from the children or a friend who is convinced that every child, no matter how well adjusted, must be in psychotherapy for hidden troubles. It is also not uncommon for self-appointed experts to be driven by their own childhood experiences and encourage parents to proceed without regard for the actual child's individual cues and needs.

The expert advice in this book is intended to work in conjunction with a parent's knowledge of his or her own child. We respect that parents are the experts on their own children, and we hope to be helpful consultants to you. You might think about it like this: parents are the pilots and we the authors are experienced copilots who have accompanied many other ill parents on this ride of parenting while sick. The ride may be bumpy at times, but your children can be delivered safely and lovingly into adulthood.

The Numbers

For many reasons, a growing number of American children are being raised in families in which a parent has a serious or chronic illness. Medical advances are picking up illnesses sooner and are keeping people alive longer. Many adults are choosing to start their families at an older age and have the medical conditions that are to be expected with advancing age occur while younger children are at home. Some illnesses, such as diabetes, breast cancer, and asthma, are increasing due to lifestyle and environmental factors. The result is that millions of parents are confronting the challenges of raising healthy children when they are ill.

The National Cancer Institute estimates that one out of every four of the 1.3 million adults diagnosed with cancer every year is parenting one or more children less than eighteen years of age.

Breast cancer rates have increased dramatically in the past twenty years, and a striking one in three women with breast cancer is the mother of a young child or teenager. Looking at the cancer data alone makes us aware that there are millions of children in households in which a parent is ill.

Data on the percentages of patients with other chronic illness who are parents simply does not exist. Illnesses such as heart disease, stroke, diabetes, colitis, HIV/AIDS, and epilepsy each affect a million or more American adults. Hundreds of thousands of additional Americans are living with multiple sclerosis, pulmonary fibrosis, rheumatoid arthritis, neurofibromatosis, cystic fibrosis, ALS (Lou Gehrig's disease), traumatic head injuries, or other medical conditions. The most conservative estimates suggest that millions of parents and children are affected. This common situation seems to be occurring without public recognition or an appropriate response from the health-care system. As psychiatrists who work with children and adults, we see every day how essential it is for parents to have the knowledge and confidence to address these challenges directly and know they are parenting well despite their own circumstances.

Our Expertise

We are both board certified adult psychiatrists and board certified child and adolescent psychiatrists. We have many years of experience caring for medically ill children and their families as consultation child psychiatrists on the Massachusetts General Hospital's Pediatrics unit.

This traditional training set the stage for our work on the Massachusetts General Hospital Cancer Center parenting program, Parenting at a Challenging Time (PACT). Recognizing the concerns that parents with cancer had about how to help their children cope during the parent's treatment, and with recognition that some parents would not survive to see their children become adults, this unique parent guidance program was initiated in 1997. PACT provides psychological and educational consultations to parents with cancer and their spouses or partners to assist them in providing the best parenting practices in this situation. Parents are encouraged to share information about their children with the PACT clinicians, who in turn educate parents about the important milestones and typical behaviors associated with the different phases of child development. Clinician and parent weave together the information about individual temperament and development to understand each child's behavior better and use this to support the children's continued healthy development. If you were to listen in on these consultations, you might be surprised by how much laughter about funny things children say or do is expressed and how often children's accomplishments are shared. There is lots to celebrate in our meetings, and we enjoy sharing those pleasures with families.

The PACT program is unique. It was intended to provide care to cancer patients only, but as the reputation of the program grew, we were asked to help families with many different medical conditions. It became clear that parents, regardless of which illness they were living with, found the approach to helping their children cope very valuable. We also worked with health-care providers, educating them about the concerns of ill parents and the needs of their children. The message we heard over and over again from our patients as well as our colleagues was that the information we provide is not easily available anywhere else, it is very useful, and they find it makes so much sense that it is hard to believe they never knew it before. These were the key reasons we embarked on writing this book.

How to Use This Book

The information in this book is sensible, straightforward, and easy to read. The book is divided into short chapters with explanatory subheadings so that you can read the parts of most interest to you. We realize that with the pressures imposed by an illness, it may be hard to have the emotional energy or time to read a whole book. Similar information may appear in more than one chapter because each section is intended to be useful on its own. If you have the time or inclination to read more, you may find that even the topics that do not seem relevant to your current situation may provide helpful information. Good parenting advice applies in many different settings. We have often been told that the guiding principles we teach for parents with an illness are also helpful to parents facing other challenges such as divorce, an impending move, or talking with their children about disasters in the world.

In a book intended to be helpful to families living with a broad array of medical situations, we have focused on the commonalities in parenting well when ill. We recognize that every medical condition or situation carries its own particular challenges. Your medical challenges are as unique as your children and family are. We hope our approach is felt as inclusive of all families without seeming unaware of these important medical differences.

We have included many examples of parents living with common medical symptoms and dealing with a variety of situations. We hope the stories of other families will make you feel you have joined a community of parents juggling demands similar to your own. We hope this feels like a virtual parents support group. You will not see the other members of the group, but you can share their challenges and their wisdom.

Person-to-person connections are always important, and never more so than when an individual is ill or carrying a heavy load of worries. We hope that when you read this book it will feel like having a chat with someone who cares about you and your children, knows something about parenting when you are ill, and has a lot of confidence in the best intentions of parents and in the amazing resiliency of children.

Much of this book might appear to be written with the traditional family in mind: a mother, a father, and the children all living under the same roof. However, we work with lots of different kinds of families and find that the approaches described in this book are useful in any family constellation involving adults and children. While some examples may not fit your family's situation, the general principles will apply regardless of the particular shape and size of your family. Situations unique to certain families, such as bicultural families or those with single, adoptive, or same-sex parents, are addressed in a number of chapters.

The two authors of this book shared the writing and editing of each chapter. The descriptions and recommendations in each chapter represent what both of us believe to be important. We have tried to re-create as much of the experience of a personal consultation as is possible in the format of a book. In our actual practice, you would be sitting with one of us, so the chapters are written using an "I" voice. For simplicity, we have written the book as if the reader is the parent with an illness. We are mindful that in reality you may be the spouse, partner, mother or father, relative, or friend of an ill parent. We hope this literary style will be understood to include all the loving adults in a child's life. Missing from the book is the opportunity for us to hear those special stories that you can tell about your child. Know that we would love to be hearing them and joining you in appreciating what is special about your child.

Our focus in the book is on a child's perspective of a parent's illness. The recommendations reflect this child-centered approach. Our patients have taught us that they are eager to learn about how a child's perspective and needs differ from their own. This knowledge allows them to face their special parenting challenges with confidence. We do not focus as much on a parent's emotional experience of what it feels like to be a sick parent or well spouse or family member, though we recognize it is important, complicated, and intense.

All the families we describe represent composites of real parents and children that best demonstrate particular experiences. We have changed information when necessary to protect the identity and confidentiality of the real families we have had the privilege of working with. Any resemblance to an individual real person or persons is coincidental.

We are fortunate to practice as part of an incredible team of clinicians in the PACT program. The wisdom in this book is truly an amalgam of the clinical expertise of our whole team, including Stephen Durant, Ed.D., Cynthia Moore, Ph.D., Susan Swick, M.D., and Karen Fasciano, Psy.D. We have had the pleasure of close collaboration with oncologists, palliative care physicians, internists, social workers, nurses, and administrators, all of whom have taught us important lessons. None of the information in this book would be possible if not for all the patients and families whom we have had the privilege of accompanying on their medical journey these past eight years. The love and dedication that these parents have shown toward their children is inspiring.

On a Personal Note

This is the parenting book I, Paula Rauch, was looking for twelve years ago when a good friend, my age and with children of almost the same ages as my own, was diagnosed with breast cancer. She wanted to know what she could do to help her four-year-old son and seven-year-old daughter. She wanted to know what to expect and when to be worried. She wanted guidance in how to be proactive to keep her well-loved children on track during a very difficult time for their family. I was impressed then, as I am now, by the complexities of achieving those simple goals. In spite of my formal training, her questions to me challenged the boundaries of my knowledge about development, illness in the family, and communication with children. My experience as a parent made it abundantly clear to me why addressing these challenges was so important. I knew that if it were my husband or me facing a diagnosis of cancer or other serious illness, we would want help to feel confident about our parenting and would need to know we were doing our best. We would also want to be reminded that the future looks bright for our children. I hope this book brings you that comfort.

Acknowledgments

This book would not have been possible without all the families we have worked with at Massachusetts General Hospital (MGH) and beyond, who have taught us important lessons about living with illness in the family. Thank you to the members of the PACT team, Stephen Durant, Ed.D., Karen Fasciano, Psy.D., Cynthia Moore, Ph.D., Susan Swick, M.D., and Marguerite Beiser, B.A., as well as the social workers and nurses in the MGH Cancer Center for sharing this work with us. We appreciate the support of our colleagues at MGH in the Departments of Psychiatry and Oncology, with special thanks to Annah Abrams, M.D., Ned Cassem, M.D., Bruce Chabner, M.D., Michael Jellinek, M.D., Bruce Masek, Ph.D., Laura Prager, M.D., Jerrold Rosenbaum, M.D., Lidia Schapira, M.D., and Lawrence Selter, M.D. For contributing to the content of specific chapters, we thank Karen Fasciano, Psy.D., for help with the school chapter, Gayun Chan-Smutko for help with the genetics chapter, and Kate Silbaugh for help with the legal chapter. Our readers and friends Anne Fishel, Ph.D., and Kate Walsh provided perspectives on the manuscript, and our editors, Christine Junge at Harvard Health Publications and Judith McCarthy at McGraw-Hill, provided tireless editing and encouragement. Special thanks go to our families, who have supported our investment in this work and who bring joy and meaning to our lives.

CHAPTER 1

How Young Children Understand Illness

Understanding the interplay between development and your child's experience of your illness will help you support your child's evolving emotional health. Think of development as the changing lens through which your child sees the world. When you understand how that lens is changing you can understand your child much better. Your child will conceptualize the same experience at each stage differently, and you will want to understand those differences. Parents are often curious about how life looks through their children's eyes, and they correctly imagine that if they better understand things from their children's perspective they could parent more effectively.

The first two chapters will describe a child's normal developmental path. Each phase of development is characterized by a set of emotional milestones that your child is striving to achieve. These milestones will be described along with the ways in which challenges posed by your illness or treatments are likely interwoven with your child's mastery of these milestones. By learning about the interplay of child development and parental illness, you will be able to better appreciate your child's real worries and needs. It will guide you in the parenting approaches that help your child stay on track developmentally and continue to grow up emotionally healthy and secure. Hopefully, you will find it fun and interesting reading.

Infancy and Toddler Years

Infants live in the moment—they aren't able to worry about the consequences of a parent's illness. New parents can feel good about focusing more on their baby's development than on their own concerns about how their illness will impact the baby's future. Learning about development will help you put your child's behavior in context and be a good parent. Many parents imagine when their infant is in distress that it is a result of their medical condition, when it is really simply an expression of normal development. With this in mind, this section is mostly focused on understanding normal development at the beginning of life.

The Beginning

Parenthood began with your first thoughts of how it would feel to be a parent and your fantasies about the baby you would have. It began long before you held your newborn in your arms. Each of us hopes to have a baby who will grow into a person who embodies the best aspects of ourselves, one who is capable in areas in which we may feel weak and one who is less vulnerable to the factors that hurt us in childhood. Similarly, each of us hopes to reenact the best of the parenting we received as children and to correct the areas in which our own parents missed the mark. Parenthood begins in the imagination—and then along comes your real baby.

It is unlikely that your perfect parenting fantasy included parenting with an illness. It is you, not your infant, who suffers with the "What ifs" such as, What if I can't breast-feed? What if I can't chase after my toddler? What if I don't get to see my baby grow up? By focusing on your baby's developmental milestones, you can be sure to provide a wonderful foundation for your child and at the same time help yourself enjoy the miracle of development in

If You and Your Newborn Must Be Separated

Some readers may have a premature infant or an infant with a medical condition separate from or related to the parent's illness. Often in this situation, the birth and brief hospitalization you had hoped to experience turns into an extended hospital stay. It is common for one of you to be able to go home first. It is difficult when your baby is ready to go home before you, and you and your baby are separated. Talk with your family and the hospital staff to work on a plan, if possible, that allows you to see your baby most days, even for a brief time. It is difficult to be separated from your baby in these early days, but humans are resilient, and separations, medical interventions, or other unwanted intrusions will not prevent the important process of attachment from occurring. You will find ways to love and connect with your baby despite the challenges.

If you are up to it, this is a great time to begin a baby journal. You can include your baby's height, weight, a lock of baby hair, photos, and perhaps a footprint. Be sure to include your experience of becoming a parent. What is it like for you? What amazes you about this little being? Your child will love reading this many years from now.

the here and now. Babies change quickly. There is lots to experience. Enjoy your child.

Your Newborn

Babies come wired with their own personalities, their own strengths, and their own challenges. (Chapter 7 describes different temperament styles.) Reality is most often different from one's imagination. Perhaps you imagined holding a big, cuddly son, and you found yourself embracing a delicate, fussy daughter. Some departures from the fantasy are welcome, interesting, and exciting, while others challenge your ability to embrace the role of parent. If your baby is difficult to soothe, has very disrupted sleep, is irritable much of the time, or has trouble learning to feed, parenting can be challenging. This is accentuated when you are living with fatigue, pain, nausea, or other symptoms of an illness. Many parents would describe any infant as challenging in all these arenas—some are harder than others, but rarely are infants really easy. You will need help, and in order to get it, you'll need to plan ahead.

The Infant-Parent Relationship

Individual differences between infants affect the infant–parent relationship, as do differences in parents. You and your partner have your own personalities, schedules, and beliefs, as well as your own challenges. The challenges may include economic distress, discord in the relationship with your coparent, a postpartum depression, or your illness. Whatever the challenges, the goal is to create secure attachments between your baby and her primary caretakers. "Caretakers" is plural, because it is too hard to raise an infant alone. Infants can have important relationships with many caretakers that lead to secure attachments and a thriving infant. As an ill parent, or as the coparent of someone who is ill, it is important to know that babies thrive in many types of loving relationships.

Creating a Realistic Support Network for Your Baby

It may be a huge disappointment to you to have to parent with a serious illness that interferes with your energy level, time spent together, or mood. But these factors need not cause suffering to your infant. As one parent told me, "When I am in the hospital, I imagine that my baby thinks I am away on a business trip. I know that at six months, she actually has no concept of a hospital or a business trip. Thinking of it as a trip makes me feel better, though. Being away on a business trip doesn't seem so scary to me."

You may feel reassured to know that separations from your baby likely seem worse to you than to your infant. The insecurity you feel about the medical situation is a worry that your baby is too young to share. Many parents have told me they find comfort in learning that their awareness means they are "suffering" more than their infant. It is comforting to think of the infant as shielded by living in the physical moment.

How It Feels to Be Your Infant

In the first year of life, babies are learning how it feels to be in the world. Your baby is experiencing his or her own physical feelings—from the pleasures of being warmly held and having a full tummy to the discomforts of gas or cold air on wet skin in the bathtub. It is not possible to keep an infant from ever having an uncomfortable feeling—and if it were possible, it would not be in your infant's best developmental interest to do so. A baby's sense of security comes in part from knowing that uncomfortable feelings happen, get better, and are not so frightening. Imagine how different a headache feels if you think it will get better soon as compared to believing it will persist unabated forever. Experiencing bearable physical and emotional challenges while feeling loved builds your baby's self-confidence and security and prepares your baby to cope with the real world, which is never free of frustrations.

Babies in healthy environments learn that enough of what is needed happens, and thus the world feels pretty good—inside and out. He or she is not left hungry too long, and not left cold and wet for too long. Your baby is learning that people who love and care for him or her can be depended upon to respond to the baby's cues and communications often enough. At the same time, your infant is learning to communicate more effectively in order to get those loving responses.

To accomplish this learning, it helps to have a small number of consistent caretakers who have enough experience with your baby to learn his or her nonverbal cues. Communication among caretakers is important. You may schedule regular talking times to share the events of the day or keep a communication book with helpful hints such as particular positions that your baby likes to be held in or how long to let her feed before burping her. What works to soothe your baby one time may not work the next, but your caretaking team will be accumulating many effective ways to soothe. Different loving caretakers may respond to your baby's distress with somewhat different approaches and at different speeds. Most babies easily learn to feel secure with these differences, and these variations can help your baby grow into an adaptable child.

But babies vary too. They have different temperaments. How often or how quickly should a caretaker respond to distress? There is certainly no perfect amount of responsiveness—the range varies for babies of different temperaments. Every time your infant cries, does that mean a caretaker needs to rush over and pick him up or offer milk? No. Does it mean that one has to pick up a crying infant every hour of the night? No. But, it does mean that your baby learns that when she is overwhelmed, she can expect to eventually be soothed, more quickly in the day than at night, and that she knows she has not been abandoned. Babies who seem to have a bit more trouble soothing themselves probably need more attention at this early age. What is being established is a gut sense that the world is a responsive, loving place. This is the opposite of an infant feeling alone and unheard, or as if attempts at communication or soothing would be hopeless.

Loving Your Child from a Distance

If you need to be away from your baby for weeks at a time, you may find it helpful to have daily check-ins with one of the caretakers at home. Ask what strategies worked that day and which ones did not. Hear about your baby's sleep and wake cycle for the day. Find out if there were any new accomplishments—rolling over, grabbing a foot, or putting her thumb in her mouth. You can be a key part of the caretaking team even when you are in the hospital. Just as important, you can also be enjoying and learning about your baby each day. You might also consider providing caring from a distance by creating audiotapes of yourself singing a lullaby or reading stories, as well as having photos of yourself with your infant readily available for caregivers to look at with your child.

Remember, even the most attuned parent cannot possibly read a baby's every cry, grunt, or body posture. Sometimes a parent may feel so guilty about the challenges presented by the medical condition that he or she imagines unrealistically that healthy parents are perfect. (My own mantra comes from my grandmother, who used to say, "If you want perfect, look it up in the dictionary, because that is the only place you'll find it.") Don't hold yourself to unrealistic standards; your baby doesn't.

Creating a Loving Environment

Though establishing the right team of caregivers is the most important thing you can do to make your baby feel secure, you can also set up a comforting environment for him or her. Your baby will learn to associate a favorite blanket, sheets that smell just right, and familiar music with the safety of being soothed and loved. Loving adults and surroundings that are infused with safety are a great combination. As your baby moves through his first year, he may become particularly attached to his blanket, a soft diaper, or a stuffed animal. These special cuddling items are referred to as transitional objects, like Linus's famous blanket from the Peanuts comic strip. Experienced parents often encourage that attachment to occur with a blanket or diaper that can be easily washed and is not a one-of-a-kind item. They know that a toddler or preschooler can be very distressed if his transitional object is missing even for a few hours. Now is the time to think about what regular cuddly blanket or toy to put in the crib at every naptime or bedtime and to make sure you have more than one as a backup.

Planning for the Unexpected

When you are living with an illness, the unexpected is expected. A doctor's visit or diagnostic test runs longer than anticipated, an urgent hospital visit is required, or an extended hospitalization becomes necessary. It is helpful to have a plan A for your baby in these situations and a backup plan B, and it does not hurt to have a plan C and D! Parents in this situation often find that they use them all.

The best way to ensure your infant's comfort is to communicate with potential caregivers about your baby's usual schedule, feeding needs, sleep setting, and the soothing techniques you know work best for him or her. It is great to write these tips down so you don't have to worry about relaying them to someone from a pay phone at your doctor's office or on your cell phone from your hospital room. They can be updated periodically and kept in your baby's room, your kitchen, the diaper bag, and with the portable crib. Little notes in cabinets are helpful too. Signs that tell caregivers that bottles and nipples are here, crib sheets there, and extra pacifiers over there all help a new caregiver hit the ground running. Another useful preparation for the unexpected is to have a diaper bag and portable crib ready for travel—with the familiar, and therefore soothing, items inside.

When Your Baby Is One

By one year, your baby is a better communicator and is physically on the go—some crawling, some cruising (upright with supports like the coffee table), and some walking or running on two feet. He or she may communicate with some recognizable sounds such as the "uh-oh" that accompanies dropping food from the high chair or "mm-mm" for food or "ba-ba" for bottle. Most communication at twelve months is by gestures, especially pointing, and crying or whole-body expressions such as reaching up with arms to be picked up, perhaps underscored with an urgent vocalization. The good news is that these communications are easier for a less familiar caretaker to decipher as compared to the different cries of a five-month-old.

The better your child is at communication, the easier it is for a friend or family member to help out without much preparation. In fact, your toddler is probably a pretty effective communicator when it comes to what he *wants*. It may not be as easy to assess what he *needs*. Your toddler is curious about a host of things in the environment—baby toys, the buttons on the stereo, a multicolored art object, his brother's toy that is being played with at the moment—and usually he is good at signaling the wish to get that desired thing. You or another caretaker recognizes your toddler's pleas for access to those objects, determining which ones are appropriate to offer and which requests should be met with a "no-no" or a redirection of attention. There are behavioral patterns that you will recognize as signaling that your child is becoming tired or overwhelmed and needs a break. For example, your toddler may request thing after thing without being satisfied with any of them. It is harder for a toddler to tell you directly that he needs less stimulation and help to quiet down, instead he will need you to help him identify this need.

Having many caretakers results in many opinions about what is appropriate for exploration by curious one- to two-year-old hands. Hopefully, when it comes to issues of safety there is little variation. You may want to review safety issues with your toddler's caretakers such as rules around climbing on the staircase, using the car seat, or playing with toys with small parts that are choking hazards. You should not feel embarrassed to state important safety concerns aloud. You need to feel confident that your child's caregiver is a safe supervisor. You may want to return home to observe your toddler's caregiver unannounced or ask a family member or friend to do so, as a way of seeing what is happening when the caregiver is not expecting to be observed. You can ask a caregiver how she handled common events such as small injuries or fevers in her previous child-care experiences. You can make up scenarios and problem solve together with your caregiver to assess her abilities and share your own preferences.

Experiencing the environment goes beyond safety, though. No caretaker will allow even the most curious toddler to play with the stove or the electric can opener, but whether a colorful heavy glass fish on display can be fingered by a well-supervised toddler may be open for interpretation. Those differences in rules begin a process of interpersonal exploration for your toddler now and into the future, as he becomes a preschooler. (*Grandpa let me hold that fish; Mom let me play with buttons on the DVD player. How come*

Grandma will not let me hold the fish and Dad says a stern "No" when I touch the DVD player?) It is okay for there to be differences between the rules set by different loving adults. It is helpful if each of those adults is pretty consistent, as it does confuse toddlers when the same person behaves differently on different days. Your toddler will be more likely to test out the rules around the things that are different person to person, but he will soon learn what each accepts. It is appropriate for children to learn that there are variations among loving caregivers.

Your toddler is answering important questions for herself, not by thinking deep thoughts, but by doing. If she points at the fish and says, "me, me, me," who will give her the fish and who will not? She is exploring the emotional question of whether the people who love her will give her everything she wants when she wants it. Hopefully your toddler is getting enough of what she needs when it is needed, but also learning that she will not get everything she wants when she wants it—as was also important during infancy.

Once Your Baby Is Two

The so-called terrible twos begin with this dilemma about what is a "want" versus a "need." Your toddler is a better communicator and knows that his caretakers understand his requests. He has a longer attention span with more persistence than he did in his first year of life. The result of all these developmental factors is more frustration at not getting what is wanted and more protest about it. That is the essence of the "terrible twos."

You may find it very difficult to bear your toddler's distress, or you may feel comfortable riding out the inevitable episodes of protest. How difficult this is varies. If your toddler has a very intense temperament, he may protest long and hard, which is difficult. If your toddler has a different temperament, she may easily turn her attention to a new interest that is allowed. That makes it easier on you.

Parents vary in their own ability to manage the feelings that an unhappy toddler evokes, with or without a parental illness. It is common for two parents to differ on this. Some parents are "softies," and others are very firm. If you are too restrictive, your toddler may not have the opportunity to explore the environment and learn from his or her curiosity. If you are too permissive, your toddler may get hurt. But the most common challenge that parents of toddlers face is being inconsistent. If you routinely waffle on what is permissible and what is not allowed, your toddler will learn to protest and protest until he or she gets the desired outcome. Parents often say, "I hate to see her upset, so first I say no, but then if she cries or wails, I give it to her anyway." This common description of the experience of trying to set limits with a toddler is usually followed by the parent saying, "I know I shouldn't give in, but she just cries and cries and I give up, because it isn't worth it. She knows I will!"

Try to be consistent. Before you say no, check in with yourself. Can you distract your toddler and redirect her? If you choose to say no, then follow through on lovingly reinforcing that limit no matter how loud the protest. It is harder for you, but it helps your toddler begin to learn to listen to your words and believe them.

Maintaining Routines When a Parent Is Sick

When you or your spouse is ill, it is easy for the caretakers—parents and nonparents alike—to become softies and let structure in the household go. Sometimes this is motivated by guilt—"His father is in the hospital, poor guy. An extra video won't hurt him." Sometimes the demands of the illness make it hard to keep to a schedule, and sometimes there are many caretakers who don't really know the toddler's routine. Rules around meals, sleep time, bedtime rituals, and playtimes may all become unpredictable and negotiable around the toddler's preferences.

At this age, your toddler cannot understand complex explanations with words, and specific amounts of time or times of the day have no real meaning to him. Following the daily rituals is critical to help your toddler be able to anticipate what is coming throughout the day and thus to feel safe, secure, and settled.

Protest notwithstanding, routines are comforting at any age, but especially for toddlers. For example, the routine could be dinner at six in the high chair, with two finger foods, followed by bath, twenty minutes of playtime, two stories, and bedtime at the usual hour. Security is having a familiar bed and caretakers who know the usual ritual. When your health care takes you away from home, this sense of routine is especially important for your young child.

No family keeps to the ritual every single day, but aiming to keep to the daily routine most days of the week is a good plan. Some toddlers will adapt better than others when there are disruptions in the schedule, and part of what you are learning is how disruptions affect your child. Sometimes a flexible schedule will cause your toddler to be upset that day, and sometimes the distress will be expressed the next day, or not until the schedule is back to normal. If the schedule is posted on the refrigerator and in your child's bedroom for each caregiver to see, everyone can work together to keep your toddler's schedule regular.

It is often important to educate caretakers about how toddlers rely on a regular schedule to feel secure. They may need a reminder that keeping to the schedule is not being unkind but rather is the most caring approach. Sometimes a friendly reminder on the posted schedule helps, too. "When Mike's regular routine is followed things feel safe and secure to him, and he wakes up happier the next day. Thanks for keeping him on his schedule!"

Building a Caregiving Team

Luckily infants and toddlers are adorable, because they demand an enormous amount of care—day and (sleepless) night. It is exhausting to parent babies! Ideally, every parent with an infant or toddler would have help with caregiving, but this is especially true when you have the added demands of your medical condition. It is important to build the best available team of caregivers for your baby. This may include paid professionals at your home or at another location, friends, family members, or all of the above. A small number of caretakers, three or four, who know your baby best as your main supports and others who can help in an emergency make a wonderful team. It is often not possible to create a complete team, but if you are working with a smaller group, expect it to be challenging and exhausting. It is important for your own sense of well-being to trust your baby's caregivers. They don't have to do everything exactly as you would, but they need to be safe, loving, and open to communication.

The Big Picture

Infancy is a time that goes by quickly, and the developmental changes are amazing. There is a popular adage that the minutes go slowly and the years go quickly. In spite of being tired, try to focus on your baby's development, curiosity about the world, and zest for life. Your baby is one person in your life who is not worried about your illness. Enjoy him or her. If you can keep a diary, baby book, or photo album, you will appreciate having it to reflect on later. Your child will too.

Preschool Children (Ages Three to Six)

Many parents say that preschoolers and teenagers are the hardest ages to parent. Your preschool child is wonderfully imaginative, chatty, and fun. He or she is also easily frustrated, often headstrong, and intent on challenging the limits that caring adults impose. Learning about key developmental factors at this age will help you adapt your parenting practices to the challenges and opportunities your young child presents when you are living with a medical condition. Children at this age really do say the funniest things. Write them down so that you and your child can laugh about them in the future!

Understanding Preschool Thinking

At this age, your child is egocentric and has immature logic that allows her to weave fantasy and reality together to explain the world around her. Being egocentric means your child can imagine the world only from her own vantage point. She might point to a picture in a storybook and ask you from across the room to identify the picture that only she can see. This is an example of your child's egocentric perspective in terms of observable physical things. She is continuing to work on the complexities of loving relationships, especially understanding why the people who love her most do not always give her everything she wants when she wants it.

The same egocentricity applies to the emotional experiences as well. When you get an important phone call from the plumber or the doctor and stop playing with your son, he may get angry at you. He might tell you that you are being "mean" to leave to take that call. From your child's emotional vantage point, it feels as if you are purposely ignoring him. He does not take into consideration that there is a leaky pipe that urgently needs to be repaired or that you are awaiting test results. He may assume that you like talking on the phone more than you like playing with him, and so he feels rejected and mad.

It is age appropriate for your child to experience everything only in relation to how it affects him directly. You can help your child *begin* to see others' points of view by explaining why you do what you do. After many interactions he can learn that your reasons for doing something may differ from what he imagines. "I like playing with you, but I also have to talk to the plumber so he can help fix the leaky pipe in the basement." But, for the most part from your preschooler's perspective, whether you are talking to the plumber or the doctor does not matter; it only matters that you stopped playing with him. Sometimes you may want to use these interactions as an opportunity to teach your child new and more accurate feelings words (described on page 31). "I am not being mean when I talk on the phone, but I understand that it makes you feel upset when I stop in the middle of our game." It may be tempting to give explanations that are too complicated or simply too long for your preschooler to understand, especially when he is mad. For example, "Don't you understand there might be a leaky valve in the toilet, and if it keeps flowing like this we are going to get a really big water bill this month? The plumber finally called me back. I have been waiting for this call all day. Hopefully he understands this is important and will get over here before five o'clock" is less helpful than "This was an important phone call. The toilet is broken. I need the plumber's help." Keep it simple.

It is not uncommon for your child to say he "hates" you at this age. But what "I hate you!" really means is "I am mad at you." Most parents find it painful to have a child say these words, but this is a good opportunity to educate your child. Simply reflect back to your preschooler the more appropriate and accurate language: "You are really mad at me!" perhaps followed by "Do you want to tell me why?"

Preschoolers use associative logic, which means that they connect unrelated information (some real and some from fantasy) in order to explain why things are as they are. A four-year-old girl might say, "My brother doesn't want a dog, because he is a boy. I want a dog, because I am a girl." It might be accurate that her brother did not want a dog, while she did, but older children and adults would not think that being a boy could explain a disinterest in owning a dog. Her explanation makes sense only through her associative logic, where any two associated facts can be connected as if one causes the other. (By comparison, her nine-year-old brother might say that he did not want a dog because he did not want the responsibility of taking a dog for walks in the rain and snow. We may not agree with his preferences, but his logic makes sense.) Associative logic prevents preschoolers from understanding that some things happen by chance. For young children, every event that occurs is assigned an imagined reason for occurring.

Why is it important to understand egocentricity and associative logic? Because together these characteristic features of preschool understanding create what is called *magical thinking*. Preschoolers believe that everything happens for a reason, never by chance or luck (associative logic) and that reason often has to do with them (egocentricity). As a result, when you are diagnosed with a serious illness your young child is likely to believe he caused the illness.

For example, when asked if he had any ideas about why his dad had had a heart attack, a four-year-old replied that he had been jumping on his daddy's stomach the night before his heart attack. "My daddy said, 'Ouch, that hurts,' and then when he woke up, he had a heart attack. Right, Mom?" When questioned further, it was clear that this little boy had connected these two unrelated events and believed he was responsible for his father's cardiac arrest. By asking him what he imagined caused the heart attack, his mother was able to correct his misconception and feelings of guilt. "You did jump on Daddy that night, and he did have a heart attack the next day, but he didn't have his heart attack because you jumped on him. Playing with kids doesn't cause a dad's heart attack." You need to be aware of your child's possible feelings of guilt, and asking some questions like this can get to the bottom of these feelings.

Playing Is Important

Preschoolers need the opportunity to play. Fantasy play, such as dressing up as different characters or playing with dolls, dinosaurs, or cars, allows your child to work out worries and safely experience a range of feelings. One can think of fantasy play as therapeutic storytelling. Children will replay important real-life or imaginary experiences over and over, often exaggerating what actually happened, adding a magical scenario, or playing the role of the more powerful person, such as the teacher or parent instead of the child. For example, a child may be heard telling her doll, "Don't worry, baby. Your mommy will come home from work *later*. Have a bottle." Or "Don't cry, baby, or you'll have to sleep outside on the sidewalk!" Another child may delight in pretending that his *Tyrannosaurus rex* defeats armies of other dinosaurs. This play lets him feel the pleasure of being the biggest and most powerful one—the antidote to being a four-year-old who resents being "bossed around" by all the caring adults in his life.

When you have a medical condition, it is not uncommon to see medical themes in the fantasy play of your child. He may play out trips to the doctor or hospital and enjoy applying bandages or giving shots. Having medical play materials available such as a toy doctor's kit or Band-Aids will facilitate this useful play. Some of your preschooler's play may be hard for you to watch. Hearing that the baby doll is crying because her mother is at work or seeing a teddy bear get hundreds of shots and Band-Aids can raise your concern. Has my life situation burdened my child? Not necessarily. When your child plays out emotionally challenging imaginary scenes that spring from his life experiences, he is engaged in a healthy developmental process. All of us face emotional challenges in life, and the capacity to manage our challenges and continue to invest in life is psychological health. If your child is calm enough to tell a story in her play, then she is integrating new situations into her understanding of life. It is best if you let your child play without trying to redirect the unfolding storyline. As tempting as it might be, it is better not to suggest to her that she tell her baby doll to be happy because the mommy is coming home soon or to tell him that teddy bears need only one painless shot and one teeny Band-Aid. Play reflects an emotional reality, not an exact retelling of real events. Your child is likely playing out the story just the right way for her own needs.

It can be helpful to listen for misconceptions in a child's play— not so that you stop the play in the moment, but to correct the misconception in a conversation later. For example, a five-year-old is driving his toy ambulance to the dollhouse saying, "Emergency! Emergency! Everyone at 6 Mantle Street is having seizures." He should be allowed to play uninterrupted, but at a quiet time later, his parent might ask, "Do you ever wonder if you and your sister will have seizures, because I do?" Giving the child in this example the chance to talk about his understanding of seizures and why they happen helps his parent understand what he is thinking about her medical condition. This allows her to understand his particular worry, and she can reassure him that he and his sister are not going to have seizures along with her.

Your Child's Body

Your preschool-age child understands his body as a whole entity, something like a large water balloon that is not made up of separate distinct body parts, but contains liquid. When a four-year-old breaks his arm, his body is broken. When an eleven-year-old breaks her arm, she knows that only her arm is injured and that her legs, her abdomen, and her head are not affected. The younger child who sees a parent walking with a cane will imagine that the parent is injured all over. He will be reassured by being reminded that even if you are walking with a cane, or if your arm is in a sling after surgery, your ears are good for listening to your child's stories, your eyes are very good for watching your child's building play, and with either one or two good arms you can give good hugs.

Your child may play that she has your disability. It is common for a preschooler to announce that like her parent, she has cancer, too. This is often followed by an enactment of the symptoms the child associates with the parent's illness. Sometimes your child is not distressed when she's acting sick, she's simply copying your behavior as other behaviors are copied. Sometimes your child may be genuinely distressed. She may be using the symptoms modeled on yours as a way of seeking extra caretaking because she has seen that others care for you when you exhibit these same symptoms or express these complaints. In this latter situation, it is important to correct your child's misconception that she has your illness, but it is also helpful to provide some extra cuddling time. "I am sorry your tummy hurts. You don't have colon cancer like Daddy, but sometimes kids get tummy aches. Do you want to sit with me for a few minutes until you feel better or until you are ready to have a poop?"

Processing Facts and Feelings

When preschoolers are trying to understand something complicated, they may talk to themselves about the topic or even sing to themselves about it. Especially when a topic is emotionally challenging, there is a tendency to separate the emotional expression

How to Involve Your Child's Preschool Teacher

It is usually the best advice to encourage your child's preschool teacher to listen to information about your illness, symptoms, or treatment with the same warm interest that she would listen to any other information from your child, but not feel that it is her job to educate your child about the illness or treatment. It is also important that the teacher greet you and your child each morning with the usual smiles and attention to your child. It is natural for the teacher to want to express concern for you, but your child will absorb a sense of worry if the once happy morning greeting changes to a solemn one. Your child may also misbehave if the attention of the teacher has switched to you instead of your child. (We will discuss collaborating with school personnel in detail in Chapter 9.)

from the cognitive understanding. So your child may be weepier about not getting her favorite color cup when you return from the hospital, but she may talk about your medical condition with no apparent distress.

Separating the factual understanding from the emotional impact is normal. For example, a preschooler may announce with pride at circle time, "My mommy had a brain tumor cut out of her and she has stitches in her head!" The absence of apparent distress can seem odd or troubling to you or to the preschool teacher, even though it is normal. Sometimes your child's teacher may also worry about the reaction of her other students. Rarely do preschool classmates bat an eye at these disclosures, no matter how upsetting the information may sound to an adult. All preschoolers are egocentric, and another child's parent being ill is not particularly worrisome or even meaningful. It is likely to precipitate the typical circle time associations from different classmates such as "My mother had an operation once," "My babysitter got a haircut," "I got stitches in my foot when I stepped on a clamshell," and so on.

Setting Limits

The greatest challenge for parents of preschoolers is usually setting appropriate limits, keeping rules consistent, and managing your child's attempts to redefine the rules and schedule. This is especially difficult when a parent is sick. Parents may be too tired to enforce a rule their child resists, or they may feel guilty about setting limits after the illness has interfered with something the child had hoped to do. It may be another supervising adult who decides to change parental rules to be "nice" or because of a different set of personal priorities.

The rules that are most consistent and therefore most predictable are less likely to be the ones that your child resists. For example, if your child is never allowed to use a very sharp knife, he will be unlikely to have a temper tantrum demanding to use one. If riding in her car seat is always required, then even if there is some period of protesting, she is likely to accept that this is a nonnegotiable rule and simply comply. It is typical for the rules that are inconsistently enforced to be the ones your preschooler protests about. Often the rules that are inconsistent surrounding a parent's illness are not safety rules, but rather rules about following schedules or acceptable behavior. For example, if one day you can be convinced to stay another few minutes at the park and then perhaps to stay another few minutes more, your child will be sure her pleading changed your mind. In reality it may be because it is the first sunny spring day or because you are eager to share news about your treatment with a friend who happens to be there, too. Your child is likely to be delighted to have gotten her way, and you may both be happy that day. The problem is that on the next trip to the park, your child cannot understand why you will not agree to the extra minutes before leaving. *Why*, the child wonders, *did you listen to me last time and not this time? Perhaps I have not shown you how much I want to stay in the park.* So she begs or cries or runs away or struggles when you try to enforce the leaving time. You have accidentally taught your child that this is a rule that can be changed if you want it to change. It becomes your child's mission to get you to renegotiate the rule. If escalating protests from your child can change your mind, he or she will learn that protest, temper tantrums, running away, or even hitting or kicking is effective. Of course, this is not the lesson you want your child to learn.

No parent should be like a robot who has rules that absolutely never vary, but ideally you should try to decide before your child's protests escalate whether to change your rule or not. For example, you might say, "You can do three more things on the play structure and then we will go to the car. Remember, if you want to get to do three extra fun things next time we come to the park, you will have to be a really good cooperator when your three things are done and I call you to come to the car." When you change the rule, let your child know that this is the case and why. "You can play longer, because Sam's mom just arrived and I need to talk with her."

The goal for parents is to set up a system of rewards or treats for good behavior. For example, "If you help me get you undressed for your bath, you can play with the bath crayons!" Or, "If you get into your pajamas quickly, I bet we will have time for two storybooks tonight!" When your preschooler resists the hoped-for behavior, you could say, "Oh dear. I hope you are going to be a good cooperator with putting on your pajamas, because you will be so sad if we don't have time for our second story tonight." The intent is for your child to learn that cooperative behavior is rewarded with special time or fun treats. Keeping things positive works better than getting into the negative cycle of taking more and more things away from an uncooperative child such as, "If you don't stand still while I get you undressed for your bath, there will be no bath toys, and no stories tonight."

Making Bedtime Go Well

It is especially difficult to be consistent when you are stressed and fatigued. The end of the day is hard for your child and hard for you, especially when there is the added burden of the fatigue, preoccupation, or irritability associated with your medical condition. It is useful to think about how to orchestrate a good bedtime experience before it's time for your child to hit the sack. It is important that bedtime features a predictable routine and that it is calm. It is helpful to be realistic about your emotional resources and those of your partner or other caretakers at this time of day. Who can best provide this calm routine? Should it be alternated, or is there another adult who can help with bedtime some or all evenings of the week? Let your child know what the night's routine will include and who will be doing what. The more predictable it becomes, the easier it is for your child to adjust. The designated bedtime parent or adult may not always be your child's first choice. Often at this age, children have a strong preference for a particular parent. Decide in advance what the plan will be and stick to the plan. Initial protest will usually give way to acceptance if protest does not change the stated plan.

It is important to recognize when the bedtime ritual is not working. There are some illnesses or treatments that leave parents particularly fatigued or impatient in the evening. If you or your partner is not able to carry out the bedtime ritual without getting angry, it is important to talk about that and make accommodations. Perhaps the fatigued parent can create a special routine at another time of the day, such as watching a video together in the parent's bed after lunch or having a special "snuggle time" after dinner. Repeating an unhappy bedtime sequence night after night is not good for you or your child.

Errors of Kindness

Another common challenge comes up when extended family members are doing a significant amount of the child care and routine. If they feel sorry for your young child because of your illness, they may want to buy your child lots of gifts or be reluctant to enforce bedtime, eating healthy meals, or keeping to routines when your child protests. The permissiveness encourages your child to misbehave in search of the security of an expectable routine. Recognizing this connection may be hard for these caring adults, and criticizing them may be hard for you when you rely on their help.

Age-appropriate limit setting, routines, and expectations convey the important message to your preschooler that the loving adults in his life have confidence that he can bear the frustration and disappointment of not always drinking from his favorite cup, or not getting to watch one more video, or going on an outing without getting a new toy. When your child learns by experience that he can manage these disappointments, ultimately he will become more confident in his own ability to cope. Learning to manage reasonable disappointments, having loving limits, and living within a healthy routine helps a child develop self-confidence. Share this important piece of education with all the adults who love your child and are helping you parent.

The Big Picture

Preschool-age children are imaginative, communicative, and full of zest as well as impulsive, demanding, and provocative. They can be charming little helpers one minute and whining, protesting obstructionists the next. They thrive in consistent and lovingly structured environments that allow them to safely explore the limits of acceptable behavior and caring relationships while learning about the exciting world around them. Though they may seem to need a frustration-free existence, it is learning to manage frustrations, disappointments, and second-choice options that leads to establishing greater self-confidence in the real world as they grow up.

Preschoolers have a way of reducing adults to their emotional level. It is a struggle, when yelled at, not to yell back. "You're not the boss of me!" "I am too the boss of you!" Few if any parents are without stories of behaving more like their four-year-old than like an adult on particular occasions. The goal is to try to stay calm, reward positive behaviors, not inadvertently reward negative ones, and mean what you say and follow through on appropriate consequences. Try to get all the regular caretakers to agree on the basic rules of the family and to see the way consistency benefits your child. Parenting cannot be perfect at any age, and this is certainly true for parents of preschool children.

Talk with other parents of children the same age and share funny stories and upsetting interactions. The camaraderie and accrued wisdom of the parenting community is a great support, and you are likely to discover that issues you might assume are related to your child coping with your medical condition also exist for the children of parents without any medical conditions at all.

Elementary School Years (Ages Seven to Twelve)

Your school-age child is entering a time of wonderful accomplishments. He or she will be learning so many new skills: academic skills such as reading, math, and science; art skills such as playing a musical instrument, drawing, and singing; and athletic and social skills. Your child will also be learning how to learn. He or she will be learning the value of practice and hard work as a means to improving all these emerging skills. You will want to support all this learning in spite of the demands of your medical care. Your child is likely to have a busy schedule that assumes your availability. When your medical treatment or illness interfere with your child's schedule, it is important to find a balance between simplifying the schedule and getting extra adult support to facilitate your child's routine.

Parental Support Is Key

Most of the activities during this phase of childhood occur outside the home. However, even the most independent child needs intensive family support to be successful. It is a parent or attentive adult who takes a child to soccer, reminds her to pack her homework in her backpack, sends her in with colored pencils for the art project, and attends the poetry reading breakfast in the classroom. When you and the network of caring adults you have organized are able to provide these supports consistently, your child is likely to take the support for granted and tune in to her own many challenges and accomplishments. It is an incredible gift to a child to be able to provide a support system that is so steady that it recedes into the background almost unnoticed.

Your child may complain that she has told you before about something she feels she needs and be upset with you that it still has not been provided. It may feel as if she is being particularly insensitive for not recognizing how all the demands of your illness make it difficult to shop. But it is useful to recognize that her high expectations are the result of how secure she feels in the love and support provided by you, your family, and friends. You will have to explain how the illness affects your family and how some expectations will need to be different. But instead of being frustrated with your child at these moments, take a minute to congratulate yourself on what a good job you have been doing.

Rules Are Important

Rules take on special importance at this age. The adage goes that for elementary school students, "Rules rule!" Following rules is necessary in order to play recess games and sports, fit in with peers, and succeed at school. Children expect teachers, other children, and family members to be "fair." Being fair means everyone follows a recognized set of rules that your child can understand. Your child will likely react with distress when this expectation is not met, as often it is not. Your illness and medical treatment, for example, cannot be counted on to follow a prescribed set of rules that your child can depend on.

Acknowledge what is unfair, disappointing, or difficult. Let your child vent his or her distress about the disappointment, but try to redirect the anger toward the illness instead of at you. Remind your child what you can make happen as a family. Be creative about second-best plans.

For example, here is how one set of parents handled a disappointing situation. A ten-year-old girl was upset that her mom needed surgery during winter vacation, so the family had to cancel a planned trip to Disney World. Her dad assured her that they would go during spring vacation instead. When spring vacation approached, her parents sat her down and explained that her mother's kidney disease had caused some additional medical problems and she was still too sick for them to travel as a family. "It's

Best Friends

During the six years of elementary school, hopefully your child will make a best friend. These special friendships teach your child what it feels like to have a soul mate. They can spend hours playing together and then beg you for more time because they are having so much fun. If your child has not made a close friendship by third grade, you may want to check with his teacher or coach to see if there is another child or two you could facilitate a playdate with to help such a friendship get initiated.

When your child does have a best friend, often the friend's house is a favorite place to go when you are not at home or when your home routine is disrupted by the medical treatment or frequent visitors. It is a good idea to talk with your child's closest friends' parents to find out if your child can stay there during times when your medical problems or treatment necessitate a backup plan.

not fair!" she complained. "You're right. It isn't fair." Her parents validated her disappointment. "We've been doing everything we can to help Mom get healthy enough to travel and it hasn't happened as fast as we hoped. This kidney disease stinks!" They talked with her about the things they could control, like what to eat for dinner, what to watch on TV, and where to go for an afternoon out together, and what they could not control, like Mom's reaction to her blood pressure medicine. They couldn't go to Florida that April, but they were able to rent a room for a night in a nearby hotel with an indoor swimming pool. They brought Disney movies from home, and she got to bring along a girlfriend for the overnight.

Hard Work Works

Your child needs to learn that when he works hard to learn a new skill, he can succeed. Experiencing mastery is essential to good self-esteem. Children who develop one or more areas of particular achievement, such as being an excellent ball player, violinist, or reader, will integrate a sense of competence that can set the stage for lifelong confidence. Self-confidence helps children weather life's challenges. Knowing that when she practices in her area of talent she can achieve at a level she is proud of is a wonderful feeling.

You can help your child have this satisfying sense of accomplishment by underscoring achievements big and small. Comments that show you are able to pay attention to the details of your child's life convey a sense of security and normalcy in spite of the illness. Some examples: "Wow! These are tough words that you spelled correctly on this test." "Watching you swim laps today reminds me of how hard it was for you to swim across the pool even one time last summer. Look at you now."

Most children have relative strengths and weaknesses. When you are tuned in to the importance of building confidence, you can usually help your child find an area of some talent and interest and support its development. That area may be consistent over many years or may change from year to year. The essential aspect is your child's genuine experience of a positive learning curve. If your child seems to have no area of interest in which she feels proud of her accomplishment, it is important to talk with other parents, her teacher, or your friends to think of opportunities and ideas for activities that could spark an interest. Some children have an easier time finding interests and activities, while others struggle even with lots of parental assistance.

Sometimes your illness and treatment may interfere with your child pursuing a developing or established interest. Recognizing the importance of special interests may lead you to seek help from other adults to go the extra bit to allow your child to continue to get to sports practice or music lessons. At the same time, you want to keep the activities to a number that you and your child can realistically manage. You want your child to be able to attend an activity consistently. Signing on for too much and, for example, missing every other dance class, is likely to make your child feel particularly unaccomplished and unsuccessful in spite of her best efforts. Unscheduled time is important too. You should not feel

that your child has to be in activities every day. To the contrary, it is an important life skill to learn how to amuse oneself without a structured activity.

Sometimes your illness or treatment may interfere with your ability to be consistent in acknowledging your child's successes. Pain medicine, for example, may make you drowsy and cause you to nod off when your child is reading you the book report that he got an A on, or it may be unwise or difficult for you to sit outside in the drizzle to watch her soccer game. It is important to let your child know that you are disappointed to be unable to be at the game, or that the medicine makes you sleepy, and that in neither case should your child be left to think that you are disinterested.

You and your child can be mad together at the ways your illness interferes in the things you would want to enjoy doing together. Expressing that frustration to your child can help foster this sense of togetherness. For example, saying something like, "I need to take extra medicine when my joint pains are really bad, but I hate when it makes me so sleepy that I don't get to enjoy hearing you read me your fantastic book report. Sometimes, I might not even realize how tired the medicine makes me. Please let me know if it seems like I don't want to listen. I am really sorry if I hurt your feelings."

Learning to Assess Other Adults

At this age, your child has lots of opportunities to interact with adults outside of the family. There are different teachers, other school personnel, coaches, religious school instructors, and the parents of your child's friends to name a few. It is important to listen to your child's comments about these different adults. "Mark's dad is really fun." "Sandy's mom used to be nice, but she yelled at us for no reason today." "Ms. Jackson, the art teacher, has favorite kids, and it isn't fair!" "Mr. Thomas hates everyone." It may be tempting to react warmly to the positive comments about other adults and to defend the actions of the adults who draw your child's criticisms without knowing the real circumstances. In either case, positive or negative, you want to know more about why your child has made this observation of another grown-up. "What makes Mark's dad fun?" Hopefully, it is not because he lets the kids ride on the hood of his car! "What were you and Sandy doing when her mother started yelling, and what did she say? Let's try to figure out what happened." It might turn out that the children were painting on an unprotected beautiful dining room table, or it might turn out that Sandy's mother has a problem with alcohol. "How can you tell Ms. Jackson has favorites?" "What does Mr. Thomas do?"

Sooner than you think, your child will be a teenager and will be spending time with adults you do not know well. During the grade school years, it is important to educate your child about what you view as the characteristics of a caring adult. At the same time, you need to determine for yourself whether this is an adult you feel comfortable to have supervise your child or is a teacher whom your child may need to be respectful toward, but who has some ways of treating children that you acknowledge are not fair to everyone.

When you are living with an illness, you rely on the network of caring adults to assist your family. If there is an adult you rely on, but whom your child complains about, seems uncomfortable with, or is afraid to be around, this is important data that you need to pay attention to and understand better. Talk to other adults, try to observe the person with other children, and most of all listen to your child. While thankfully it is only a small number of adults who abuse children, the best way to protect your child is by letting her know that you want to hear about her experience with adults, whatever the adult's job or status, and take what you hear seriously.

Sometimes complaints about other adults in your child's life are her way of telling you she wishes it were you rather than that other adult who was, for example, taking her to soccer practice. Often as a result of your medical situation, you need other adults to do things, like carpooling, that you might wish you could be doing yourself. This may be part of why your child is complaining. He wishes it were you doing the drop-off at school, not a friend's parent. Uncovering your child's unhappiness with the substitutes for you gives you an opportunity to let him know that you care about the impact of your illness on him. You may be able to prioritize your time to be able to drive him to practice once a week, or it can be just as valuable to your child that you acknowledge that your illness and treatment are hard on him and you feel sad about that reality.

Talking About Feelings

Seven- to twelve-year-olds are maturing emotionally and learning to use language to express the full range of feelings. It is wonderful when your child feels excited, proud, and happy. But it is especially important for your child to learn to cope with strong, difficult feelings such as anger, frustration, embarrassment, and sadness in safe and healthy ways. Your illness may be one stressor in your child's life, but there are also many other challenges she will face during this phase and through life. Being able to express her feelings is essential to getting her needs understood and met.

You can help your child by first encouraging him or her to develop a rich emotional vocabulary. Be a good model yourself. Take the opportunity to describe your own emotions. "I am disappointed that it is raining and we can't go swimming." "I am so frustrated that it took so long at the hospital today. My appointment was at 1 P.M. and I didn't see my doctor until 3 P.M." "I was nervous about doing a presentation at work, and I am proud of myself that I did such a good job in the end." When your child is displaying behavior that you think reflects a set of feelings, you can try to name those feelings for him. "I think you were disappointed that the coach didn't let you play as much as you had hoped." "I can tell that you are upset about our decision not to let you go to that movie." "I think you are embarrassed that you forgot one of your lines in the play, but I don't think the other kids or parents will remember that part." When you suggest a feeling that your child may have experienced, be open to having your child correct you. "I wasn't embarrassed that I forgot that line. I was mad, because I said it right every time in practice."

Look for opportunities to compliment your child too. "I know how disappointed you were when I told you that you couldn't go on that sleepover tonight, but I am really impressed that you were able to tell me your feelings without throwing things or yelling." Let your child know that you expect her to have a mixture of feelings about your medical condition and treatment. It is normal to sometimes be angry at or embarrassed by your parents, but it doesn't feel good.

You can make learning "feelings" words a game. Keep a list in your child's bedroom of words that describe different feelings as you find them in the books or poems you read together. Express interest when she finds an unusual word to show you. Let her add

People Who Love Each Other
Get Angry at Each Other

You may feel more on edge because of the illness, fatigue, uncertainty, and financial stress or needing to be in too many places at once. It is important to model healthy ways of being angry and of reconnecting after anger has been expressed. Avoid name calling such as "Quit being a baby" or "You are such a slob!" Long after the situation has passed, your child is likely to remember that you called him a "baby" or a "slob" and feel angry or ashamed.

Help your child to weather his own angry outbursts without hurting himself or hurting anyone else, without breaking his things or anyone else's. Together you can establish ways of apologizing for words or actions that are regretted and acknowledging that the love between you is not threatened by the episodes of frustration, anger, or disappointment.

new ones that she finds herself. Encourage your child's school-teacher to include these emotional words on the weekly spelling list. There are many variations of a poster you may have seen that includes rows of cartoon faces, each expressing and identifying a different emotion. Hang one up in the kitchen and encourage your child to use the words from the poster to express herself.

How Your Child Understands Illness

Your child is likely to have a pretty simple understanding of illness. Most of what children this age have learned firsthand about illness is about viral illness, like the common cold, or perhaps bacterial illness, such as an earache or strep throat. At home and at school, they have probably learned about germs causing illness and the importance of washing hands, putting tissues in the trash, and covering one's mouth to cough or sneeze. Many serious illnesses are not contagious and are not spread by touching or a sneeze. If your child is not at risk of catching your illness, you need to let her know this. The unspoken worry about this could be causing your child to pull away from you.

When there is a known cause of your illness or condition, whether it is genetic such as cystic fibrosis, or chronic obstructive pulmonary disease from smoking, or a head injury from a car accident, your child may be relieved to hear that the illness happened for what seems to him a logical reason. It also means that perhaps she can envision a way to protect herself from getting the same medical condition. There may be some comfort to your child from being able to see a connection between an action and a medical condition.

Still, no one deserves to get lung cancer even if she was a smoker, nor a spinal cord injury because he was driving too fast on a rainy night. If your child hears other adults or children minimize the impact of your illness because of an action or behavior that led to the illness, your child is likely to feel upset or angry. Asking her about what she is hearing will help you find opportunities to understand her worries better, educate about misconceptions, and remind her that no one deserves to get a serious illness.

Simple explanations about treatment help. If you are engaged in an active treatment for your illness or condition, you should give your child a simple explanation of what the treatment is and why you are receiving it. If the treatment causes symptoms, it is helpful to explain which of the symptoms you have are from the illness and which ones are from the treatment. If your treatment schedule is predictable and has an expectable impact on your functioning, your child will adjust better when he knows the schedule of treatment and resulting symptoms. "I will be getting my chemotherapy every three weeks. I will circle my treatment days on the calendar. On those days, I will be really sleepy, because the nurses will give me some special medicine to help me not get too nauseated from the chemotherapy. That medicine makes people sleepy. Dad will be in charge of homework and bedtime on treatment days."

Being a Helper Can Help

At this age, your child is learning lots of new skills. You can ask your child to do some simple tasks that help you or the family. Different families have different expectations about chores for children. Age-appropriate chores could include putting dirty laundry in a hamper, making his own bed, setting the table, or taking out the trash. A smaller number of expectations that are consistently expected is usually best. The goal of chores is to teach your child to take pride in his ability to make a difference in the family. To promote that goal, it helps when you underscore how what he has done helps you or the whole family function better or feel better. "It's a big help having you take out the garbage." "I appreciate your help setting the table. I enjoy having your company in the kitchen, too." It's hard to feel helpless at any age, and sometimes a chronic illness makes family members feel helpless about making a difference. Asking for help and appreciating the help you get is good for everyone.

The Big Picture

The key developmental tasks for children in grade school include experiencing how hard work leads to a sense of personal accomplishment and close friendships build self-esteem, recognizing how caring adults treat children, and learning how to express and manage the full range of feelings, including anger, as an essential part of maintaining quality relationships. When you know what these key developmental tasks are, you can facilitate opportunities for your child to master them in spite of the demands of your medical condition. Sticking to your child's regular routine and paying attention to the details in his life contribute to an overall sense of security and normalcy.

Children this age need to know the name of your illness and are usually reassured to hear a simple explanation of the condition and the treatment plan and why the latter is being instituted. They likely have a simplistic understanding of the cause of illnesses and will benefit from hearing what did and did not cause the medical condition and whether it is something that they can "catch." It also helps to clarify what symptoms they notice are a result of treatment (such as hair loss with chemotherapy) and which are genuinely a sign of advancing medical condition (such as becoming wheelchair bound in ALS). Your medical illness, even if it is a serious one, can usually be managed in a way that keeps it from interfering with your child's exciting, expanding life.

How Older Children Understand Illness

Even after your child looks physically mature, he or she is still on a steep developmental curve. It can be particularly challenging to remember that your adolescent or young adult child who looks so mature is emotionally not functioning like an adult. Greater developmental understanding helps you have more realistic expectations of your older child and paves the way to maintaining a better relationship. It also offers you the opportunity to consider what information about your illness will support your child's need to manage greater independence and increasing demands at school or at work.

Talking about the developmental principles in consultations with parents of children in any of the age ranges often leads parents to smile and nod with recognition of many familiar behaviors, experiences, and parenting reactions. Hopefully, you too will have this experience of recognizing aspects of your child in this chapter, which can help you both weather the challenges of parenting your older child and enjoy the experience.

Adolescence

Your adolescent is undergoing an amazing transformation. His or her body is changing, and it is a time of identity development and aspiring independence. It often feels like a teen has an easier time rejecting parental values, or criticizing the behaviors or ideas of adolescents in other cliques, than knowing exactly who she is or what she believes in. During this time, the norms of dress, behavior, and activities of the teen's peer group become the key yardstick, and parental viewpoints are frequently seen as out of date. Moodiness is common. Sexuality is in the air, and intimate relationships are being explored.

When parents discuss their illness or treatment with their teenagers, it is common for the teens to seem to understand it as well as any adult. However, the ability to discuss a parent's medical situation rarely translates into a teenager demonstrating consistent, appropriate behavior in light of the demands the illness places on the family. That disconnect between understanding something in what seems like a mature fashion and behaving without the same maturity is a normal part of adolescent development, but it is one of the greatest challenges for parents living with an illness.

Changing Bodies

It is common to grow several inches during this phase and for your child to become physically mature. Adolescent physical maturation is highly variable so that at fourteen years old, your child might appear more like an eleven-year-old or might be able to pass for a nineteen-year-old. Looking much older or looking much younger may present particular challenges for your child. But, even if your child looks age appropriate and attractive in your eyes, he or she is likely to feel ill at ease and unhappy about at least some aspects of adolescent appearance.

The physical changes in conjunction with hormones and sexual attractions contribute to feelings of self-consciousness. Common teenage girl preoccupations include body weight, breast development, bad hair days, and dissatisfaction with facial features. Teenage boys often worry about being short, less muscular, or hairless or about their penis size. Both girls and boys are troubled by acne. Sometimes these common preoccupations seem to be heightened by the teenager's general feeling that things at home are not as secure because of your medical condition. Often, teenage girls get annoyed with friends or classmates who are preoccupied with these small worries when they are worrying about an ill parent and family stress.

Cognitive Changes

Physical changes are the easiest to see, but the cognitive changes under way are just as dramatic. Your child's ability to consider multiple possibilities and their consequences emerges during this phase of development. This is a cognitive capacity that is referred to as abstract thinking and enables him to think about such weighty topics as philosophy, politics, human rights, and the meaning of life. Your teenage child is able to comprehend the uncertainty associated with an illness with a poor prognosis and the potential of a future without you. This new sophistication in thinking and its expression in complicated discussions or debates make the often impulsive and self-absorbed behavior of adolescents perplexing. It is as if they both "know" and "forget" the implications of serious illness and other issues of magnitude.

There are reasons why teens cannot seem to apply that complex thinking in their real lives. First, there is so much going on inside them and so much changing around them. There are also so many conflicting and exciting peer opportunities facing them. Because of these things, it is rare for teens to be able to consistently focus on the needs of the family.

It may also be difficult for your adolescent to make safe choices, including those that relate to drugs, alcohol, and sexual activity. This can be frustrating, upsetting, or frightening to parents. How can a child who sits at the kitchen table and honestly describes clearly all the reasons why drinking and driving is dangerous and unacceptable be the same child who does just that after a party? Unfortunately, the cognitive ability to think abstractly about many possibilities is not typically associated with equally well thought through behaviors and actions. The best approach for helping your teenager is calm, open communication without being angry, blaming, or expressing too much disappointment. Often, it is very hard.

Establishing an Identity

Adolescence is sometimes referred to as the second separation. The first separation is when a toddler learns to walk away from her parents. In this second separation, the child is striving for independence and attempting to establish a new and genuine identity separate from her parents. This normal process may complicate your relationship with your child. Teenage identity can be likened to the hollow chocolate bunnies that are sold at Easter— elaborately decorated on the outside, but not solid on the inside. Teens are often preoccupied with exactly the right outfit, hair, and attitude but at a loss to tell us what really matters to them. Sometimes, it may be your illness and the uncertainty that surrounds your health that lifts your teen out of the typical adolescent concerns to identify family health and safety as a core priority. Sometimes, that uncertainty leads your teen to throw himself into other activities as a way to keep the worry about your illness at bay. Often both are true at different times.

Parent-Teen Relationships

Your thoughtful child, who used to ask your opinion about how to handle difficult situations, may now be a teen that doubts your ability to understand the current social situation or academic demands that must be negotiated. Your strong-willed child may now be a teen who is difficult to communicate with at all, getting exasperated with your advice or rules almost before you complete the first sentence expressing your viewpoint. While it is usual to have a mixed relationship with parents at this age, it is also important that there be some sense of connection. It is important that when your teenager feels most stressed she can come to you or her other parent for support.

It is common for a child to feel closer to one parent than the other. This may be a gender issue such as a girl finding it easier to talk to her mother, or a temperament issue in which a child with a fiery temper does better with the parent who has a mellower temperament and can more easily defuse a situation. Sometimes the difference in comfort between your teen and you or your coparent is small, but other times it may be extreme. If your child feels completely alienated from your healthy coparent, this may make uncertainty about your long-term health particularly anxiety provoking or make her feel especially alone when you are engaged in treatment that takes you out of the home or renders you less emotionally available. If this is the case, it is best to talk about it openly with your child. "I know that you and Dad have a harder time talking together. What could he do that would make it easier for you while I am getting rehab every day?" Let your child know that your coparent also recognizes that it is difficult and wants it to be better. If you can get each of them to try something small, like having tea together in the morning or trying to talk together during the car ride to school or an activity, this can help establish an improved connection. Letting your child and your spouse know that you would feel better if they could improve their communication by 5 percent can set the stage for a modest but noticeable change. If they are completely at odds with each other, it may be best to agree on another family member, counselor, or friend to rely on as your stand-in during these stressful times.

Important Adults Who Are Not Parents

It is normal for teenagers to attach to nonparental adults—a favorite teacher or coach, an extended family member, or a friend's older sibling or parent. Often these caring adults can make the same suggestion to your child that you have expressed, but it is easier for your child to take this other adult's advice. When your teenager is looking to adults you consider good role models for support, you are lucky and are being offered an opportunity worth seizing. Encourage those relationships, and when possible let those special adults know key information about your illness, treatment, and family situation. It is not easy to be a teen or the parent of a teen. We can all benefit from quality adults who aren't in the immediate family taking a part in our teens' lives.

Around the House

Your illness or treatment may necessitate that each family member pitch in. If you have been living with the illness for a long time, and your teen has been expected to do certain chores and assume additional responsibilities, the transition to adolescence may go more smoothly. However, when the rules in the house change dramatically in adolescence, your teen may not take immediately to these changes. For example, when you expect a teen who has never had household tasks to do dishes, do laundry, take out the trash, and babysit after a new diagnosis or reinitiation of treatment, your teen may often "forget" her jobs and disappoint you and your spouse. Commonly, some of what is expected of the teen gets done, but it either is not consistent or requires lots of reminders, and that can be annoying or make you feel that she is inconsiderate or even hurtful considering the difficult circumstances of your illness.

Only when you cannot do all the usual tasks does it become clear how much you were really doing when you felt better. You may not have realized yourself how many little things you could do when you were fully mobile or had your full energy, including zipping out to the store to pick up the one thing that was needed for dinner or school, throwing an extra load of laundry in the machine, picking up the wet towel on the bathroom floor, returning a sweatshirt to the appropriate bedroom, or putting away the remains of a late-night snack.

Even when adolescents are capable of completing each of these seemingly simple tasks, they are not likely to be able to take over the "executive" function of assessing what most needs to be done in the house and doing it. Discussing which tasks need to be done, using charts, and anticipating a degree of lack of completion are helpful. For example, you might have a weekly calendar that lists one chore for each day of the week. If you have two teenagers, one could be assigned washing up after dinner and the other taking out the trash from Monday through Friday on alternating weeks, each assigned to clean his or her own room every Sunday, and one to do the laundry on Mondays and the other on Thursdays. The weekly chore chart should include a space where your child can check off the completed tasks. The structure of the chart provides clear expectations—"It's Monday, don't forget to do a load of laundry"—and when completed without a prompt, it is an opportunity to thank your teen for his helpfulness. "I hear the washing machine going; thanks for your help, it makes a big difference." You might also be alert for the child (usually a girl) who takes on too much around the house, to the exclusion of more age-appropriate activities with peers that are important to her social development.

One of the predictors of good family coping during a child's adolescence is expecting teenagers to be moody and messy and not seeing this behavior as abnormal or purposefully inconsiderate. Often what is most upsetting are the things that we expected to be different. Expect messy and moody and your teen is likely to provide you with many pleasant surprises.

Peer Relationships

Hopefully, your teenager has a group of friends with whom she associates and who help her define herself. High schools are often divided into multiple groups with each group having its own unofficial dress code, designated favorite activities, and even a special location in which to congregate at school or outside the school. Adolescents rely heavily on their peer group for processing worries, for helping them explore newfound independence, and for establishing intimate relationships. Teenagers vary in how private they choose to be about a parent's illness. Most will find support in sharing this with at least one or two close friends, and some will be very open with a wide range of friends.

It is important to try to get to know your child's friends and, if possible, some of their parents. This is more difficult as your child gets older, but it is just as important as at earlier ages. If your teen's peer group is engaged in dangerous behaviors including using drugs and alcohol, selling drugs, or stealing, you will want to discourage these relationships, and likely you will need to get help from your child's guidance counselor, pediatrician, or a mental health provider. If, overall, the friends seem like good kids who treat your child well, encourage your child to stay involved with them. Even if you do not like the teens your child is choosing to spend time with, it is important to try to understand what your child sees in these teens.

One teenage girl shared with her mother that she preferred being with the "outcast" girls, because she thought they understood her worries about her mother's cancer better than the popular girls. This helped her mother recognize that her daughter felt alone with her worries. She made an effort to invite her daughter to talk about her experience more often. They agreed that she would see the school counselor for a while, because the girl admitted she worried about burdening her mother with her worries. Her mother encouraged her to bring her favorite female friend to their home for dinner regularly, and both girls got involved in a social action club at the school that eventually led to some new friendships.

If you are lucky enough to have a relationship in which your teen talks with you about his friends, hearing about their experiences gives you an opportunity to learn about the challenges and pleasures facing your child and his peer group. Be a good listener, and encourage your child to share his view of why peers behave as they do. Try not to be too judgmental, but do share your family values as they relate to the situations you are hearing about. Some teens that are reluctant to talk about themselves will talk freely about other teens they know at school. You may want to ask if your child knows of classmates who have an ill parent. If so, your teenager may be willing to talk about the stresses this other child faces or how that family situation has changed the other child's behavior. After fully exploring this, you may wonder with your child about what is the same or different about his experience.

School

Your teenager is functioning in a complex school environment. In the early grades, there is usually one teacher who oversees your child's school experience. In middle school and high school there are typically many teachers, and rarely is there an opportunity for all of a child's teachers to compare notes. This can allow a significant change in a teen's school performance to occur without any one teacher seeing the pattern unfold, and without you knowing until the end of the term. It would be much better to learn about your child's school difficulties as early as possible.

Particularly because you probably have a lot more on your plate than parents who aren't dealing with an illness, it is useful to seek a "point person" at the school to check in with your child's teachers and let you know if he is skipping classes, not handing in homework assignments, or doing poorly on tests. Your child may have strong feelings about what information you share about your medical situation with the school. It is best if you and your teen can come to some agreement about how much to share and with whom. (See Chapter 9 for information on communicating with the school.)

In these higher grades, teens are expected to do reading and writing that demands good concentration and attention. Worries about your illness may affect both, and thus interfere with school functioning, or may simply lead your child to feel entitled to put academic drudgery on a back burner as it seems a low priority by comparison. By recognizing a school problem quickly, you can work with the school to consider appropriate accommodations and seek academic support or counseling for your child.

Risk Taking

Adolescents are known for feeling invulnerable. One teen who was in a drunk driving accident later talked about how he felt "bulletproof" after a couple of beers. It is hard for an adolescent to believe anything bad can happen to him. Accidents and injuries seem to happen only to other people. Many teens have access to cars, alcohol, and drugs—sometimes weapons, too. Any of these alone or in combination can lead to serious injuries or even death. Your illness may add to the reasons your child engages in risky behaviors as an escape from daily anxieties. All parents of teens need to be watchful about dangerous behavior and seek professional help as needed.

Depression and Anxiety

Teens are also at risk for depression and anxiety. Parents of all teens need to be attentive to the signs of depression, and studies show that teenage girls who have a sick parent are at additional risk. Sometimes it is apparent when your child is depressed. He stops participating in activities and rarely goes out with friends. Her sleep habits and appetite change. Your child may tell you about feeling depressed.

At other times, your child may not want to worry you and so may hide the distress. Your child may be spending more time listening to music alone or staying up late, but this may seem like typical adolescent behavior, not the onset of depression. Similarly, your child may be struggling with so much anxiety that it is interfering with school and friendships, but it may seem like she is doing fine and simply choosing to be around the house more and being helpful. It is best to ask your child about anxiety and depression. Letting your teen know that you want to know what he or she is feeling is the first step. Seeking professional help is important. (See Chapter 13 about when to seek mental health help.) Having an ill parent can be stressful, but your teenager does not need to be anxious and depressed.

The Big Picture

Adolescence is a time of dramatic developmental changes. Teens are experiencing profound physical changes and less apparent but equally profound cognitive changes. They are beginning to look like adults, and though they have some adult thinking capacity, they also tend to make decisions guided more by emotion than common sense. Their peer relationships take on a new intensity because the group a teen belongs to defines so much of his sense of who he is. Dating becomes more intimate, and self-esteem is affected by how a teen is viewed by the person he or she has a crush on or is in a relationship with. This is the backdrop against which your teenager is experiencing your medical condition. Your adolescent is confronted with more challenging expectations at school. Even without an illness in the family, many high school students feel overwhelmed by these demands. Your adolescent can fall behind if emotional distress associated with your medical condition interferes with her concentration. Keeping school staff apprised of your situation is important.

With so much going on in your teen's world separate from you and communication at times more strained, it is common to feel in the dark about your teen's experience. Many parents find their teens self-absorbed and are deeply disappointed that they do not help more around the house.

Knowing what is normal teen behavior helps you to set realistic expectations for your relationship with your teen. As with younger children, talking with other parents of similar-age children and experienced teachers can provide helpful perspective on your child's behavior and good ideas for ways to help your situation. It also lets you be aware of signs that your teen might be getting involved in troubling, risky behaviors or displaying symptoms of depression or anxiety and need professional help.

Late Adolescence and Early Adulthood

Parenting is a lifelong task. You are still a key person in the life of your late adolescent or young adult child. Some people describe adolescence as continuing until your child is thirty! This section is intended to highlight the issues for the older child who is beginning a first full-time job or is attending a post–high school educational institution. For simplicity, I will refer to this time in your child's life as young adulthood.

Beginning Adulthood

At each phase of your child's life, it is easy to see how a stable family situation provides a solid foundation for your child's new experiences and challenges. This is still true for your child who is entering adulthood. The transition to college or to a full-time job is often very challenging. Your child is being assessed by a new, different, or more demanding set of expectations. These may include reliability, good humor, and good decision making at a job or higher academic standards and time-management skills at a college. Transitions are always complicated and often stir up doubts. "Am I able to do a good enough job to satisfy my boss?" "Am I smart enough to be here?" "Do these new people like and respect me?"

When facing new challenges it is nice for your young adult child to be able to return to a safe home base in which he or she can feel loved, respected, and understood. Your home and your young adult child's longtime friends offer that haven from new challenges and self-doubt. If you have a newly diagnosed illness or if your medical situation is changing, it is especially hard for your child to leave home with a sense of security. By talking openly about your illness, establishing a plan for sharing information, and recognizing that your young adult child may need to check in more often, you can facilitate a more secure transition.

Serious Relationships

Your young adult child may be involved in a more serious intimate relationship at this age. He may be relying on this new soul mate to provide the security and nurturance that was previously found in your family. This special boyfriend or girlfriend may be a wonderful support when the relationship is going smoothly or may multiply the distress your child feels about your medical condition when the relationship is disrupted. Whether or not a parent is ill, these serious relationships may be a source of comfort to parents or a source of concern.

If you imagine this person your child loves is good for him or her, you may feel that your child has a helpful partner to face life's challenges. Many parents describe the introduction of this special young person into their family as a welcome addition at a stressful time. Other parents describe a girlfriend or boyfriend who is unreliable, often disappoints their child, and seems to be a poor choice. When this is the case, the parent may worry that the stress of his or her medical illness has contributed to the young adult child making a "bad" choice.

It is not possible to control the relationship choices of your child at this phase of life, but you can use the lessons learned from your illness as a way of highlighting the qualities you hope your child's ultimate partner will embody. Tell your child about the best characteristics of your supportive spouse, close friends, or extended family such as reliability, willingness to help out with chores, empathy, nurturance, and so on. Let your young adult child know that these are qualities you want her to have in her life partner.

Talking About Your Medical Status

You may want to protect your young adult child from the full impact of your evolving medical condition. You may want your child to be free to make decisions about where to attend college, what community to live in, or what work opportunities to pursue without taking your health into consideration. This is a common extension of parental love and concern, but it is not fair to your young adult child.

A young adult is integrating all the complexities of life circumstances and making choices that respect what he has learned about his own values and coping style. Your child needs to know about your health status to know if she wants to be an hour from home or across the country. Many college students, for example, will report how important it is to know they can return home easily and see how a parent's health is in order to be able to fully invest in their academic and campus life. Other young adults will talk about organizing schedules or opting for work assignments that allow them the comfort to know that they can spend unscheduled time at home without undue impact on colleagues or job performance.

Your child needs to have the facts about the challenges ahead for you in addition to the demands of the new setting for her. One complexity is the uncertainty that you and your family live with when you have an illness. Often you cannot predict what your medical status will be later this year, or certainly for the next four years. At this age, your child can understand this uncertainty, though this does not make it simple. If you do not talk candidly about your medical status with your older children, you leave

Freshman Year of College: A Particularly Challenging Time

Freshman year of college for your child who lives away from home can be especially challenging. Academically there are fewer hours of classroom work and much more reading and unsupervised learning than in high school. Often your child will be sharing a small dorm room with another teen, and rarely do they become soul mates. Often her freshman year roommate is not a good match in terms of sleeping pattern, socializing, or degree of tidiness. Many freshmen will stay awake until very late, the dorm halls may be very noisy, and many of them will not attend meals regularly. It is often a surprise to freshmen how much they feel at loose ends when no one knows them. Teens define themselves in large measure by how they are viewed in their peer group, and your child may have left all or most of his friends when he began college. It can be exciting to have the opportunity to redefine his identity at college, but also very unsettling. If your child's high school friends knew about your illness and treatment, it may be hard for your child to adjust to no one at college knowing about this important part of her life. Some parents feel that once a child goes to college, they cannot speak to anyone at the institution, but this is not so. With your child's permission, letting the freshman dean know of your medical situation and any significant change in your health status is appropriate. If your child is feeling particularly worried or alone, the freshman dean can be a point person for getting additional help or having a place to check in.

them alone with their worries about your health. They may make uninformed decisions that they later regret. Your child may either feel compelled to be close by to assess you because he or she is not confident that you are being open and honest or may choose to be far away and later wish he or she had had more time with you. When one lives with uncertainty, it is probably better to plan for the worst-case scenario in order to minimize regrets, and then hope for the best scenario to occur. In general, it is important to provide young adult children with the information they need to make an informed decision, without burdening them with parental agendas about their future.

Communication Still Matters

The approaches to communication described earlier apply to older adolescents and young adults as much as to younger children. Being honest, exploring questions, encouraging your child not to leave worries unexpressed, and finding the settings in which open communication is most comfortable are all essential. If your young adult child is not living at home, you may need to utilize additional modes of communication such as e-mail, scheduled phone calls, or parent-child dinners in your community or his. Carving out designated times that encourage all forms of sharing allow you to hear what is happening in your child's life and to share what is happening in your own life. Most parents will find that they and their adult children are most happy if the parents do far more listening to their children's experiences than talking about themselves. This is as it should be, but it is important to invite your child's questions about your health or other family issues too.

In particular, if your medical condition has the potential for changing considerably over weeks to months, it can be helpful to set up some guiding principles about when your child can count on updates from you. For example, you might plan a call to your twenty-four-year-old working in another city the weekend after doctor's visits or diagnostic testing to share the latest assessment and treatment plans. You might discuss with your college sophomore that you expect to have testing done at the end of the semester and would rather talk about it after exams when she is at home. That is a reasonable plan only if your daughter agrees to it. If she tells you that wondering what she will hear from you after exams will be more distracting than getting news during the week before finals, you need to respect her wishes.

If changes in your health status are likely to occur suddenly, then talking openly with your adult child about how quickly he would want to hear about a serious event or who she would want to have call her if you were hospitalized is helpful. If you have been living with your illness for a long time, you may have had previous experiences that you can use as examples. "If I suddenly get readmitted to the hospital, should I wake you up with a call at night or wait until the morning?" "Is there a number I can call at work so someone can locate you wherever you are that day?" You may not be able to implement the exact plan you craft together, but it will help you and your spouse or other key adults know what would respect your child's wishes and coping style. Children of any age may become quite upset when they learn that a parent was hospitalized days earlier, but they were not informed until the parent's medical condition was stabilized.

Talking About Money

Young adults may be concerned about family finances and not express that concern, or in contrast they may be completely unaware of financial stress that is significantly impacting the family. Your young adult child may already be shouldering some of the financial responsibility for his own life or may soon be expected to do so. It is hard for a young adult to manage money if he or she has not been educated about the real costs of an adult life. It is wise not to shield your adult child from family financial issues and not to leave these issues cloaked in mystery. Frank discussions are most helpful.

When families can provide a financial buffer for young adult children, the transition to living independently is easier and less scary. Many parents, however, with or without an illness, are not financially able to provide that extra help. Most children will appreciate hearing that you wish you could make it easier for them, even if you are not able to do so. In the final analysis, it is your loving understanding more than the money that provides your young adult child with a secure foundation.

Your Young Adult's Impact on Your Younger Children

When your young adult child leaves for college or gets her first apartment, your younger children may feel the impact of the transition more than you realize. It is helpful to check in with your younger children and find out if they have worries about how the family will function now that their sibling is not at home. Your children may have a different perspective on what tasks your older child was performing in the house. Hearing from them what feels different and reassessing chores and responsibilities will help your younger children feel understood and supported through this transition. Sometimes this turns out to be a wonderful opportunity to recognize that the youngest child is no longer too young to have some responsibilities, and chores can be more evenly distributed among all the remaining children at home.

Floundering

Many young adults have a difficult time getting started in life. Some children have always seemed a little less mature than others their age, and they may be moving toward work or school at a slower pace. Still, if your child is living at home and not attending college and not working steadily, it can be worrisome.

Your child may be less eager to transition to a more independent life because of your illness and concern about how you and other family members will manage if she leaves. If this is the case, it is important to talk about a plan together. If it is a transitional plan in which your child wants to be at home for six months or a year while you receive treatment, this may be a choice that your child feels really good about making and one you can support. But an open-ended decision to put her life on hold may not serve her well. More often your child may have issues that interfere with this transition that are separate from your illness and care. Trying to understand what your child wants for himself and perhaps finding mentors in the community that could help your child pursue possible interests can provide stepping stones to bridge your child's transition into adulthood. Talk with other parents, teachers who knew your child well, and other adults your child may be close with to explore ways to help him get engaged in a job or a training program.

Making it easy for a young adult to live at home for free and not work or attend school does not help your child prepare for life. It is difficult to activate an unmotivated young adult, but it is crucial to try. If substance abuse is part of the problem, it is likely that your child will need referral to get additional help. Talk to your child's doctor for help with referral sources. (See Chapter 13 for more information on seeking professional help.)

The Big Picture

Good parenting helps young adults, too. This phase of life presents new challenges. Intimate relationships often begin during this time, and the emotional intensity of these experiences may be even greater when a parent is ill. Strong connections with parents and quality communication facilitate a young adult's ability to become independent. Parents can play an important role in helping their children ride the roller coaster of strong feelings by being available as a sounding board and stabilizing force.

Leaving home for the first time is made easier when the young adult knows he will be informed about important events occurring at home in his absence. Particular attention must be given to ways to help a young adult recognize what information about a parent's evolving medical situation would be helpful as he or she decides on a college or first job and how to integrate this information into his or her decision-making process. It may be hard for parents to share information about their medical situation because they worry it will interfere with their older child's ability to be independent. To the contrary, establishing supportive patterns of communication that continue to respect a young adult's need for information supports this transition.

CHAPTER 3

New Diagnosis: Organizing Your Support System

The shock of a new diagnosis can be overwhelming. If you have been struggling with unexplained symptoms for some time, there may be some relief in putting a name and a cause to what you have been experiencing and moving forward with treatment. When the diagnosis is sudden or carries uncertainty about your survival, it may be difficult to imagine how you and your family will cope. Different illnesses will bring a range of challenges depending on whether there is a sudden event or the slow development of symptoms, and the extent of your disability. This chapter will focus on practical ways that you can organize your family and medical activities to minimize disruptions to your children's lives and keep them feeling as secure as possible as you manage your medical condition. Getting help with routine tasks will help you stay focused on maintaining the quality of your family life during this challenging time.

Gather Medical Information

In order to plan for your family, you will need as much information as you can get about the expected course of your symptoms,

Checklist for Organizing Your Support System

Use the following "to-do" list to help you organize your support system as outlined in this chapter.

- Gather medical information
- Use familiar caregivers and routines
- Ask your child's friends' parents to help
- Designate a "Minister of Information"
- Designate a "Captain of Kindness"
- Delegate mundane tasks
- Help your helpers with schedules, lists, and labels
- Ask older children what they need help with

the amount of time and energy it will take to engage in treatment, and any expectable side effects to treatment. Your medical providers can be most helpful to you if you let them know about specific concerns you have related to your family. For example, if you are the primary driver in the family, will your medications or treatment interfere with driving? For how long? When exactly should you expect to lose your hair during chemotherapy? How fatigued might you be during an acute phase of illness? Should you have relatives stay with you to help with young children? What is the expected recovery time for this surgery?

Your medical provider may have patient information booklets that address your condition. There are also associations, foundations, and organizations for many conditions that offer information and support for people with the condition and their families and medical providers. The websites of some of these organizations are listed in the Resources section at the end of this book, and you can find others by typing the name of your illness into an Internet search engine. A reference librarian can also help you locate Internet resources as well as books and other resources.

You may want to ask your physician for recommendations on the best websites. Though the Web is an incredible resource, not all the information found on websites is accurate. It is always best to check out the information you find with your health-care professional.

By educating yourself about the specifics of your medical illness, you will be better able to field your child's questions and provide appropriate answers. Some sites provide information specifically geared to answering children's questions and offer age-appropriate language for explaining your illness to your child.

Use Familiar Caregivers and Routines

The resources you and your family use on a regular basis will continue to serve you well as you deal with your illness, but they may need to be adapted to new circumstances. Familiar routines and adult caregivers will be reassuring to your children, and so you should maintain them as much as possible. The carpool may need to be used more days a week, or the babysitter who took care of your children during an occasional evening out may now become a more regular after-school sitter. Weekend visits to Grandma may turn into having Grandma stay in your home for a few weeks. It is also important to create an emergency backup plan for unexpected events that might require a different child-care plan.

For example, you might provide a contact list of other caregivers to each of the child-care providers, so that they can arrange for backup directly if you are unavailable. Older children should also have a list of contacts they can access for help. An extra set of house keys in a designated place is also useful so people can help your children get their things or be comfortable in their own home in an emergency situation.

Ask Your Child's Friends' Parents to Help

There are certain tasks, especially for school-age children, that are best taken care of by a friend's parent. For example, ask a classmate's parent to help keep track of school activities so that being the only one who didn't bring something for the bake sale doesn't embarrass your child. You may not have the energy to bake cookies, but with some notice, you or the person doing your shopping can pick some up at the store. If the children are asked to bring in paper towel rolls for a science project, the designated parent can set aside an extra one for your child too. If the children are good friends, this parent may also be the default pickup and playdate when necessary, and your child will enjoy the extra visit.

Designate a "Minister of Information"

As you gather information, there are likely many other people in your life waiting for updates on your condition. At first, you may want to talk with people yourself, and they may want to express their concern directly. Over time, however, or if you have a particularly large family or concerned community, you will need help managing the flow of information. Identify a close family member or friend to be your "minister of information." This person can spread the word among your relatives, or a colleague can provide e-mail updates to coworkers, so that you do not have to repeat yourself or have people ask awkwardly how you are doing. Let your minister of information know what information about your illness may be shared and which details you prefer to remain private within your immediate family. The minister of information can also direct people who express a desire to help out to the "captain of kindness" (described in the next section), who can let them know what help is needed.

For people that you do want to talk with directly, ask that they call you while the kids are at school or after they have gone to bed so that conversations about the illness don't interrupt family time or bedtime routines. Don't hesitate to let the answering machine get a call that comes in during dinner or to let your minister of information return calls.

There may also be a role for someone to organize visits to you at home or in the hospital so that you don't have to repeatedly explain that you are too tired for a visit or that you need some quiet time with your family. This person can let well-wishers know the best times to visit or whether you would prefer a brief phone call or note during certain times.

Designate a "Captain of Kindness"

Depending on your illness, the community in which you live, and how public or private you are about your condition, there may be a significant reaction to news of your illness. As much as you may appreciate people's good intentions, it can be an overwhelming job to field both their reactions and their wish to be helpful. If your circumstances have led many people to volunteer various kinds of

Refer Well-Wishers to Your Captain of Kindness

You're at the supermarket shopping while you try to imagine how you are going to get your child to an activity the next day because you have a doctor's appointment that could run late. When you run into someone you know in the community and she asks if you could use any help, you blurt out that a ride for your child after school would be fantastic. The mom blanches and apologizes profusely that she has other commitments during that time slot. After a couple of awkward exchanges like that one, you might stop asking for help.

If you have a captain of kindness, you could thank the mom in the supermarket for her nonspecific offer, direct her to the captain of kindness by saying something like, "Thanks, people have been great. We still need help driving kids to certain activities, though. Molly Jones is organizing all their help. Could you check with her to see what's not covered?" This way, you don't have to ask and be rebuffed, and the well-wisher can follow through by calling Molly Jones or not. If she does, she can be directed to do something that would be genuinely helpful and appreciated.

support, we recommend appointing a "captain of kindness" to organize the well-wishers. Your captain of kindness is a point person who acts both as a buffer and as an organizer of the acts of kindness. There are some people who love interacting with every caring member of the community, but most people find doing so emotionally draining. It would be a shame for your family not to have the valuable help offered by friends, family, and your community, and a captain of kindness can guide the support into truly useful directions.

When acquaintances say, "Please let me know what I can do," you may be tempted to respond with a polite, "Thanks, but we're all set." Being able to refer them to your captain of kindness, who has a list of things you need assistance with, can provide well-intentioned folks with an opportunity to take care of a specific task and feel helpful to your family. You may have several captains who take on different tasks, or a central person might stay in close touch with you about what you need. A parent of a student in your child's class could help schedule carpooling and playdates for days that you are having treatments. Your next-door neighbor may be the point person to organize who will bring meals on what days. One family, for example, found that they were exhausted by having to entertain every person who came over to deliver a meal exactly at that evening hour when everyone was tired and frayed. So their neighbor put a cooler on the porch and instructed neighbors to leave the meals whenever was convenient. This helped everyone feel calmer around dinnertime.

Delegate Mundane Tasks

While you may be used to managing your family's life quite independently, you might find that during an illness there is just not enough energy or time to do everything you used to do. As difficult as it may be to give up control over some aspects of your daily life, you may need help to accommodate regular trips to the clinic or to recover from surgery or an acute flare of an illness.

There are certain things that will be important for you to continue to do as you are able, such as participating in the bedtime
ritual for a young child or attending a special sports event. However, there are many things that you may want to do, but are a
drain on your energy, that can be readily done by others, like certain household tasks, routine shopping, laundry, and driving to and
from after-school activities. You may take pride in maintaining
your garden or lawn yourself, but asking a friend to take over
those tasks for a while may be better than struggling to do it yourself or watching the weeds take over. Relatives and friends are
often happy to help with a range of mundane tasks if they know
that they are taking care of something important to you. Let your
captain of kindness know what would be helpful so he or she can
let people who have offered to help know what is needed. Your
children may not be happy about the changes in some routines,
but they will appreciate your being available for quality family
time and special events.

Help Your Helpers with Schedules, Lists, and Labels

If you are having other people spend significant time in your
home, a few lists and organizational aids can go a long way toward
keeping things running smoothly. Caregivers and your children
alike will be grateful for calendars of children's activities, phone
numbers of contacts, or lists of what needs to be packed in a diaper bag or backpack. Labels on kitchen cabinets can help with
unloading the dishwasher or serving your child a meal with just
the right dinosaur plate and sippy cup.

I sat with a mother in the hospital who was directing her sister by phone to the locations of things in her kitchen. We sug-
gested that as this was happening, her sister label all the cabinets
with their general contents so that the other family and friends
coming to help would not have to make the same call to Mom
while she was receiving inpatient treatment.

Chapter 4 describes how to use written schedules of your child's daily routine and weekly activities to help caregivers maintain your child's familiar routine. Writing things down both makes things easier for the helpers and helps maintain consistency among your child's caregivers.

Ask Older Children What They Need Help With

Young children take for granted that adults will be there to feed them, bathe them, and take them places. School-age children may have more individual notions about what is most important to them or what needs to be organized around the house. They may have priorities about activities or mealtimes that you can take into account in your planning. They may also be more cooperative with changes if they have had a hand in making difficult choices about what gets done and what doesn't.

A nine-year-old girl whose mother was unable to drive during her medical treatment really appreciated her parents talking with her about her after-school activity choices. They sat down and explained that Mom couldn't drive for six weeks while she was taking a particular medicine, and Dad needed to continue to run his small business. This child had been signed up for dance lessons, soccer, and weekly piano lessons, and even with help from friends it might be difficult to get her to all these activities during this time. The girl told them her dance class was preparing for a recital she didn't want to miss, so together they decided that she would continue to go to dance class but give up playing soccer this fall and start up again in the spring.

Adolescents will certainly have their own ideas about organizational priorities. It can sometimes be frustrating for parents to find that teenagers can talk a good game about what needs to be done but may have trouble following through on doing any helpful chores around the house. Countless parents tell me about their high school student who understands that someone has to do the laundry and take out the trash, but when he or she is asked to do those things, is always too busy on the computer instant messaging friends, or heading out to meet someone at the mall. Then the same teen complains about not having a clean pair of jeans! Keep in mind that this disconnect between talk and action is quite normal for teens, who don't yet have the full capacity to think through consequences or abstract ideas, especially when their own desires are at stake. You may need to be patient with your teen's age-appropriate self-preoccupation, and then provide concrete expectations about give-and-take in the family. Ask your teenagers specifically what they need help with, and think together about how to balance their own needs and the needs of the family.

A divorced mother who was receiving daily radiation treatments in a different state on weekdays had a fifteen-year-old boy and felt guilty about being absent during the week and then unable to drive him to all his various events during the weekends that she was home because of her fatigue. Her son complained that he was missing important social events with his peers and thought it was unfair to have to be home on weekend nights. He and his mom sat down to discuss the fact that her out-of-town treatments were only for six weeks and that she missed seeing him during his usual comings and goings during the week. The son prioritized a few special events—a school dance, a friend's birthday celebration, rather than every movie outing—and Mom agreed to drive him to a few events and arrange for his father to drive him to others. With this arrangement she got to spend a bit more time with her son, and he got to attend most, but not all, of the activities with his friends.

Take One Day at a Time

Organizing your supports during a medical illness will be an ongoing process that will change with the course of your illness and the evolving needs of your family. Remember to stop and check in with yourself and your family members about how things are working, and reorganize as necessary. Be gentle with yourself when you cannot anticipate every need. There may also be much to learn from families who are further along in the illness process about specific ways that they have coped and what may lie ahead for your family. While every family's situation is unique, there may be wisdom in the experience of others that you can discover through local support groups or websites about your specific illness.

Maintaining a Child's Daily Schedule and Family Routine

From infancy, your child has been learning about life through being a part of your family. It began with being lovingly held, fed, and comforted. Your baby learned the secure feeling of loving arms, a familiar crib, and a full stomach. These earliest experiences provided the foundation for experiencing the world as safe and loving. As children get older they continue to rely on regular routines, familiar loving settings, and attentive parents to feel secure. They also learn powerful life lessons from how family members treat each other, what activities are shared, and how you communicate with each other. Your medical situation provides an opportunity to impart important values about how to face such challenges with love.

Each child in your family has an established daily schedule that has evolved to be appropriate for his age, interests, and the shared needs of the family. A child's daily schedule includes regular sleep times, mealtimes, and activities. Some very young children spend most of their day at home, while other children of the same age spend many hours of the day in a child-care setting. Most older children will attend school outside their home. Some will be engaged in several after-school activities, while others will spend most or all afternoons in unstructured time at home or in their neighborhoods. Whatever your child's usual schedule, it is an important source of stability and security for him or her. When most of a child's schedule remains predictable and familiar in spite of the changes surrounding your illness, life feels reassuringly normal.

Reestablishing Normalcy

In the initial days following a new diagnosis or an unanticipated medical situation, it may be difficult to attend to maintaining each child's usual schedule or your family patterns. Disruptions are unavoidable, but returning to regular routines at home, at school, and in activities as soon as is reasonably possible will deliver the message that life is returning to normal despite your illness. Even a child old enough to spend many hours of the day, or even weeks, away from home depends on predictable family routines. Familiar surroundings, familiar smells, favorite foods, family rules, and family routines all contribute to that sense of stability. Children need to know who will be at home to receive a phone call, how to reach a parent who is not at home, and who to call if an unexpected problem arises.

Reestablishing normalcy may require a number of adaptations such as a child's friend's parent driving her to an after-school music lesson or athletic practice, or having an aunt come to stay to provide afternoon supervision or meal preparation.

Many children will indicate that disruptions in the family routine are more troubling than any particular information about a parent's illness. One eleven-year-old boy complained that the hardest thing about the time when his mother was in the hospital was that his grandmother told him he could no longer ride his bike to his best friend's house to play. A nine-year-old girl complained that any one of her mom's four sisters might be at their house when she got home from school and she never knew who would be in the kitchen when she walked in. Changes in who is routinely in your home, who answers the phone when your child calls from school, or who is doing the tasks that used to be yours—especially when your child discovers these changes by surprise—deliver a disquieting message that anything could happen next. That message makes your illness seem more serious and unpredictable, and maybe more scary, too.

Breaks in the family routine are inevitable. But if, more times than not, the family still eats dinner at 6:30, lights out occurs at the usual time, and Thursday is still laundry day, and if children are included in discussion about potential changes (and the reasons for them), then it is likely that your diagnosis and treatment will seem more manageable to your children.

When your child is able to attend school prepared for the day, has opportunities to maintain existing friendships, and can continue in favorite activities, the familiar daily routine often feels like an oasis from worries about your medical condition. Your child may complain about the adaptations necessary to keep individual schedules and family routines on track, but instituting these changes provides the message that you think your child's daily life experience is important and you have confidence in his ability to continue with previously established patterns.

Your Child's Daily Schedule

It is useful to write down a schedule for each of your children. For an infant or toddler, this schedule may include naptimes, a feeding schedule and current food choices, usual bedtime, and any activities during the week. If there are babysitters or child-care providers who have already been involved with your child, you may want to explore the possibility of increasing time with these caregivers in an ongoing way or flexibly according to your needs on a particular day or week.

For older children, it is often useful to think about a weekday schedule and a weekend schedule. The weekday schedule may include the time to be outside for the bus, what needs to be in a child's backpack each day, and after-school lessons, practices, games, and so on. Putting the schedule on paper can help you be better organized yourself, and it can be posted and used by your child as an aid to his own daily organization. A posted daily schedule also serves to assist family members, friends, or a hired caregiver who may be called upon to get your child ready for school or supervise after-school time. Even if this caregiver does not get everything exactly right, the schedule may help her ask appropriate questions and conveys to your child that even when you are not present you are mindful of his needs. (See the daily schedule in Figure 4.1 for ideas.)

Some parents find calendars helpful organizers. All activities, school assignments, and important deadlines are listed on the family calendar. It becomes the shared responsibility of the child and the parent to get key information in this one place for all to see. As one mother said, "I tell my kids, if it isn't on the refrigerator calendar it doesn't exist!" This mother had intended to use the family calendar to keep track of her children's activities, but her ten-year-old son asked her to include her scheduled medical appointments, too. She was surprised by how helpful he found this.

Your Family Routine

No matter what stage you are at in your diagnosis, it's never too late to think about your usual family routine. If you have been newly diagnosed with an illness or your condition has recently changed, think about the household routine before these developments caused major changes. If you have been living with a medical situation that has been more or less stable, identify what is predictable about the household schedule and how your illness affects that schedule in ways you like and do not like.

First, consider family activities, including those that are daily, weekly, and seasonal. Do you eat breakfast or dinner together? Do you have family time after dinner? Do you have a regular pizza or pasta night? Is there a favorite TV show that the family watches

FIGURE 4.1 Sample Weekday Schedule

Weekday Schedule for _____ **(insert child's name)**

Activity	Time	Notes
Wake up		
Morning ritual		
Breakfast		
Pack backpack for school		
Leave	Ready to leave: Out the door:	
Come home from school		
Welcome home ritual		
After-school activities/ playdates		
Homework		
Unwind time		
Bedtime ritual		

together? Do you have a take-out night or video rental night? Do you attend religious services on a particular day? Do you go skiing on winter weekends? Do you have a regular summer vacation spot? Do you spend certain holidays with extended family locally or at a distance? You may be well aware of some of these habits, and there may be some you don't generally think about. Figure 4.2 shows you an example of one family's schedule for the week.

FIGURE 4.2 Sample Weekly Schedule

	Monday	Tuesday	Wednesday	Thursday	Friday	Saturday	Sunday
Eve	Piano 3:15		At Emily's, drop off 5:30				
Mike	Swim team, pick up 5:00 (We drive)		Swim team, drop off 5:30 (Tim's mom)		Swim team, drop off 5:30 (Rob's dad)		
Isaac			Dinner here 5:30			Arrives at 10 for weekend	Back to his mom's at 4 P.M.
Dad	Dad home late						
Mom			10:00 A.M. appt. Dr. S & blood tests				
All of us	Pizza night	No visitors		Pasta night, no visitors	B'ball game 7:45 at high school	Picnic (can bring friends)	Church 11 A.M. Video night, Eve's choice

This family also kept a monthly calendar that showed vacations, birthdays, and holiday visits with family. Predictable family rhythms are great for children. They are the soothing background music for your family life.

Once you have a clear sense of your established family patterns, decide which regular events you can try to maintain. You will want to balance the demands of your health needs with family priorities and with the individual schedules of each of your children. Living with an illness makes it easy to forget routines unless maintaining them becomes a real priority. Many family patterns are easy to keep up. Holding on to your Tuesday pasta night can be easy if you delegate tasks, or having a Friday or Sunday video ritual might help provide a low-energy, relaxed evening each weekend. The predictability is comforting to your child, and it can make parenting less stressful by reducing the number of decisions you need to make and relieving pressure to come up with new ideas.

Get input from your children about favorite family activities. Maybe your child will say her favorite time is snuggling with you and watching Saturday morning cartoons at home, or maybe he will say his favorite is the Saturday morning trip to the dump or washing the car. If your child can tell you about a favorite regular in the family routine, you can make a mental note to try to keep that activity in place. Some families have photo albums of routine and special family times. Paging through an album with your child may help him talk about favorite activities with you.

Keep Communication Open

Be sure to ask your child to let you know what she has noticed is different since you became ill or your treatment changed, and encourage her to let you know how those changes feel to her. For example, elementary school children often say that the biggest change since a parent's diagnosis has been the food delivered to the house by friends. Sometimes this is reported with enthusiasm, especially about brownies, cookies, and cakes that were not part

Family Activities to Consider

The following list will help you consider family activities to preserve or institute. Talk to your child about which activities he or she enjoys, and consider which family times are most important to your child and to you.

- Designated family meals (Friday night supper, Saturday breakfast, Sunday dinner). Weekly meal routines work best when the menu is predictable. For example, challah and roast chicken may accompany lighting the Friday night candles in a Jewish home, or a Sunday pancake breakfast may include the children helping mix the batter and choosing whether to add blueberries, bananas, or chocolate chips.
- Church or synagogue. Continuing family attendance at a worship service delivers the reassuring message to your children that in spite of your illness you feel connected to your religious beliefs and to that familiar community.
- Special activities (going to an athletic event, movie, and so on). As a family, you may have a special team you follow and attend games when possible. It's great if the whole family enjoys this, but if not, this may be a great activity for one parent to enjoy with one or more of your children.
- Movie night (video with popcorn). Make a weekend evening, perhaps Sunday, family movie night. Let children take turns choosing the video of the week.
- Take-out night. Make one night a week take-out food night. Let each family member have a turn to choose Chinese, Mexican, or pizza.

of the family's usual diet but now appear regularly. After some time has passed and when the food continues to be provided by others, it isn't unusual for a child to talk about not liking the unfamiliar foods that have become the norm. He may say he hates casseroles or she may say that other people's macaroni and cheese

- Breakfast for dinner night, pizza night, pasta night, or other favorite family meal night. Younger children often find breakfast for dinner fun and funny, while parents may find it easy. Pizza or pasta are easy to prepare and are often children's favorites.

- Sleepover night. Many 7- to 14-year-olds love to have sleepovers with friends. For example, choosing two Friday evenings a month when friends can sleep over or when your child can go to a friend's for the night can create special dates for your child to look forward to.

- Extended family visit day. Some families have relatives who live in the same town; others may have family members who live in an adjoining state or a few hours' drive away. Setting up special visit times when favorite aunts, uncles, cousins, or grandparents visit you or having your children visit them can be fun and strengthen family ties.

- Picnic, park, drive, or hiking day. Choose a couple of weekend days a month to enjoy nature. Go for a walk, pack a picnic, or enjoy a new playground.

- No visitors at our house days (for example, family only on Tuesdays and Thursdays). Many children complain that a parent's illness leads to too many visitors at their homes. They may appreciate having some days, for example Tuesday, Thursday, and Sunday evenings, as times when no adults can come over to visit. This can help your child feel that home is private and calm.

doesn't taste right. They miss the familiar tastes and the normalcy the meals you made represent. Our society seems to focus so much on each new fad, it can be easy to overlook how much children thrive on comfortable, familiar old things. Make a point of asking your child's opinions.

On top of holding fast to established routines, many families create new rituals after adjusting to the illness. Here are some wonderful ideas from the families I've known:

- Lying outside and watching the stars together
- Holding weekend picnics
- Visiting baseball stadiums
- Learning about different breeds of dogs by visiting kennels
- Using a motorized scooter to accompany a child on bike rides

Having a shared "mission" unrelated to health care can be fun for every family member and can create wonderful memories.

Family Meals

A common theme among professionals who work with children is the value of family dinners. If you don't regularly eat together as a family, you may consider trying to do so at least a couple of nights each week. This is a wonderful opportunity for regular communication and offers a way to update your children about potential changes in scheduling and routines. For example, you might try to start eating together Tuesdays, Thursdays, and Sundays. The weekday dinners could be used as a time to catch up on the goings-on in each child's life, and the weekend meal could be used to focus on anticipated events that will impact the family in the upcoming week.

The dinners need not be fancy, and they need not be long. What matters is that everyone takes a break from the hectic pace of daily living and sits together. This delivers a message that the family unit is important, and so is communication. Carving out time for family dinners shows that being together as a family and talking together is as important as after-school activities, athletic events, and work meetings. Family dinners seven nights a week may be unrealistic. You need to be able to be flexible about everyone's schedule and needs. Dinner table discussions need not focus

on your illness very often. Some dinners may be serious, but more often than not most can be lively and fun.

Quiet Evening Time

Quiet time after dinner is also valuable. This may include a bedtime ritual for younger children and homework time for older children. You can use this time to check in with each child one-to-one. Find out what is on his or her mind. Usually it will be unrelated to your illness, but occasionally this may be an opportunity to deliver updates about your health status or be the time when your child asks you questions. It is also a common time for a child to share a nagging worry.

Turn Off the Telephone During Family Time

Part of making family time special is focusing your full attention on your children. This is their time with you, and it should not be spent talking with friends, relatives, or other adults. It is especially important to let the other adults in your life know what specific times, like from after school until bedtime, are not the time to call with questions about your health or for updates on tests, treatments, or future plans. If your home is to feel like a safe haven for your child, then the home "airwaves" should not be filled with illness talk. When parents are repeatedly updating other adults on health-related matters, it can seem to the children that sickness is constantly the focus. These conversations also increase the likelihood that children will overhear confusing or worrisome medical news. It is much better for your child to hear such information during direct conversations between you and your child, not by overhearing explanations directed at others.

When Your Child Wants to Be Everywhere but Home

Many older children, especially teenagers, will want to be out with friends or engaged in back-to-back activities. Sometimes this has been their routine prior to your illness, and sometimes this represents a change. As parents, it is best to decide which family times are optional and which ones your child must attend, whether at home or a family outing. There is no right amount of time for a child to spend with family, but it is best if you have clear expectations that you share with your child. You will want to listen to your child's viewpoint on what is fun, interesting, and age appropriate for him. It is important for children to have strong connections with their friends and to be engaged in activities outside your home as well as to have meaningful family time. You will want your expectations for your child to take into consideration the potential that if your medical condition worsens, your child may look back on this time and wish that she had spent more time with you. This is an important consideration for you, but you need not share this thought with your child. It is not in your child's best interest to give mixed signals about spending time away from home. Try to make clear decisions that support a balance between family time and time with others.

Here are two family situations that illustrate the importance of being decisive about family time. In one family, the mother angrily told her teenage son that he could go skiing with his friends and miss the family tree trimming party, but that she was sure that if his father died before next Christmas the son would always regret it. He told me that if she had told him not to go, he would have accepted her decision. His mother told me she wanted him to maintain his outside interests and relationships, but she felt he would spend no time with his father if she did not push him to do so. On that particular occasion he did stay home, but he still felt guilty. On other days, he went out and felt guilty then too. From his perspective, he felt like his mother never wanted him to do anything away from home. She said she was just trying to prevent him from having regrets. By giving the mixed message that he "could" go out, but that he would later regret his decisions, she unintentionally increased the likelihood of future regrets and made him feel guilty and resentful in the present.

In contrast, another family with two teenage daughters communicated a clear message about family time. The parents made a standing rule that Sunday daytime and Tuesday evening were family times, unless there was something unusually special happening outside the family. When their mother died, the older daughter expressed regret about not having had more family dinners with her mother. Her father was able to remind her of all the dinners and other quality time they had spent together and to underscore that more dinners together would not have protected her from feeling sad and missing her mother. He also reminded her of how much her mother wanted her to be out with her friends and enjoyed hearing about her activities outside their home.

Parents Living in Different Households

If you are coparenting with another adult who does not live with you, your children are already used to differences in household routines and, likely, parenting styles. A parental illness can strain even the most smoothly running system, however, and will require you and your coparent to work extra hard to maintain a sense of stability for your children. Be sure to establish an efficient way to communicate about changes related to medical treatments, and have backup plans for the unexpected. If the visiting schedule needs to change, try to let children know why there needs to be a change and how long it will be in place, or at least explain how decisions are being made. For example, "Mom is not feeling well right now, so you'll be staying with me for a while. We aren't sure how long it will be, but she is going to try a new treatment to help her back pain, and we'll see how she is feeling by next weekend." Let your children know how hard it can be to be flexible with this uncertainty, and appreciate their feelings about it.

If children will be moving for a substantial amount of time, anything you can do to keep some things consistent—bedding, special toys, daily schedules, food—can help in this difficult transition. Regular visits with the ill parent in either home should be arranged as well.

Get on the Same Page About Communication

If you and your coparent do not live together, there may be discrepancies in the information you share about your illness. Your children may become much more familiar than his or her other parent with the specifics of your medical condition and everyday function. It is important for the adults to be clear about what is going on with one another so that your children are not in the role of transmitting information or of keeping secrets between households. I have worked with families in which young children have to bear the burden of explaining to one parent what is going on with the other parent's illness. On the other hand, there are other families in which the child is not allowed to say anything about the parent's illness because the ill parent doesn't want the other parent to know anything about it. In the setting of a conflictual divorce or separation, be particularly mindful of not putting your child in the middle of your personal conflicts with his or her other parent. The burden of feeling that they have to pick sides or take responsibility for a parent's anger or hurt feelings can exacerbate children's distress about a parental illness. Sometimes professional counselors can provide useful guidance in managing communication between coparents. (See Chapter 13 for help finding a mental health professional for your family.)

Make sure that all the important adults in a child's life know what language is used to talk about the illness (see Chapter 5), and be thoughtful about welcoming all questions about the illness or the changes in the family, but defer an answer until you can check with the other parent when necessary.

Sharing Your Home

If your treatment necessitates changes in how the rooms in your home are used, you'll want to think about how this will affect each of your children. For example, when you have an additional person living in your home, like your mother or a nurse, you have to find a place for her to sleep. Or you may need to move your bed into the living room to minimize or eliminate the need to negotiate the stairs or because a hospital bed is needed but does not fit in your bedroom.

Many patients describe the lack of privacy and noise as among the most challenging aspects of hospitalization. Your children likely feel similar stress when they must share your home with new caregivers, family members, and well-wishers.

If you can allow your children to remain in their own bedrooms, this is helpful. Teenagers especially need some privacy and may find it very challenging to share a room with an extended family member or sibling. However, this is not always possible. When a child needs to share his room, talk about ways to lessen the intrusion and encourage your child to voice the particular aspects of sharing that are most difficult. Doing so may lead to a better plan and a child who feels more respected and understood. One child's room may most easily accommodate visitors, but if you are housing a series of family members or one is staying for an extended period, try to find ways to distribute the burden of sharing among the family members.

Sometimes the den or family room is sacrificed, so you might want to think about ways to make another space or part of a room a more comfortable "hanging out" area. For example, you may be able to designate your bedroom as a quiet study space during early evening times when you are not in your room yourself, or be able to put a rug, easy chair, and television in an unfinished basement.

Different Children, Different Families, Different Needs

Remember these are suggestions to help you think about how to preserve a sense of normalcy in your child's individual schedule and in your family routine. When these important aspects of a child's life are consistent, it conveys a sense of stability and security. There's a lot you can do to keep things consistent, including:

- Help each child choose among favorite activities and time with friends to create an individual schedule that leaves enough time for schoolwork, best suits your child, and can be reasonably supported under your current circumstances.
- Make your home environment predictable, loving, and child-centered by maintaining familiar routines and rituals.

- Think about family time realistically, and protect special time together when possible. Take stock of preexisting important family routines, and consider adopting new ones that facilitate communication, comfort, and fun.
- Turn off the phone during key family time, such as dinners, in order to convey the message that your children deserve your full attention and interest.

Although many potential family routines are described in this chapter, you should not feel guilty about not instituting new rituals or even maintaining all the preexisting ones. Feeling guilty about disruptions won't help you or your children. Focus on the positives and what you can do. Talk about what makes your family a great family to be part of, and help each of your children feel good about relationships and activities at home and away from home. What are the things that have stayed the same in spite of your illness? Remind yourself, and your children, of how much is unchanged and how you can enjoy good times together in spite of your illness.

CHAPTER 5

Communicating with Your Child About the Illness

You and your family have no doubt developed your own style of communication about things large and small. You have lived with each other's individual ways of talking or not talking, nonverbal communications, and coping with emotionally charged issues. Think back to how you've managed other family issues: a move, a change in a parent's work schedule or child-care arrangements, conflicts about space as children grow, or changing financial circumstances. You've likely already learned from your experiences and know something about how your children best handle information and change, or how you wish you could have done things differently. A parent's illness, like any important issue in the family, needs to be discussed in a thoughtful way to help children cope as well as possible and not be left alone with their worries.

Everyone Deserves to Know What Is Going On

It is natural for you to want to protect your child from pain or uncertainty. In some families, a general style of open conversation will lead you to talk with your children about the illness just as

83

you would talk about all kinds of changes in the family. There are also many families in which parents don't want to talk directly with children about an illness, thinking, "What they don't know can't hurt them." However, my experience with children and adults who have lived through a parental illness has convinced me that in the long run, this silence may not be as protective as you hope it will be. Almost all children, even the youngest, know that something is happening—and that they are being excluded. The changes in the everyday schedule, your physical appearance, and the emotional climate in the household become apparent to them. While it is important to try to maintain the children's usual routines and preserve family time, children are best able to do this if they understand something about the illness and why things feel different around the house. A child's worries about unspoken changes can be scarier and more painful than talking about it and having opportunities to ask their questions as they arise. Research on children whose parents have cancer supports this. These studies show that children given specific information about the illness and opportunities to discuss it may have less anxiety than children who are not so informed.

Many things can be effectively communicated nonverbally or through actions in a family. But an illness is so complex and fraught with anxiety that not putting words to it only serves to leave children alone with their possible misconceptions and concerns. Even in families or cultures that do not prioritize open discussion between parents and children, I recommend that parents give explanations about the illness to prevent misunderstandings and to help children cope. As soon as children can talk, they deserve to have some language to use to describe the illness, just the way you use age-appropriate language to describe and teach them about other things in the world.

Euphemisms Can Be Confusing

You need to begin by giving your illness a real name. Even though unfamiliar words like "colon cancer," "diabetes," or "multiple sclerosis" may sound frightening at first, your children need to know the real name for your illness. Your five-year-old may not get the syllables just right, but she will overhear those words, and you don't want her to be confused about whether "breast cancer" is the same thing as the "lump" that you have described to her. Your ten-year-old may worry on hearing the term "leukemia" that now you have a new, more serious illness than the original "blood disease" that you told him about. How is your three-year-old to know that the "boo-boo" that you have inside you and requires you to go to the hospital for special medicine is not the same kind of boo-boo that he gets when he falls down and scrapes his knee, or like the ear infection that means he needs to take pink medicine? You may worry that your sixteen-year-old will take the medical term for your illness, do an Internet search, and be frightened by what she finds. You ultimately cannot protect your older child from information, but you can open up the channels of communication so she brings questions to you and receives information grounded in the reality of your medical care and your life as a family.

The Worst Way to Hear Something Is to Overhear It

I have learned from experience with many families that as careful as you may be to talk about your illness only in private, your children are bound to overhear things. Whether it is in those first few days after a biopsy when you are on the phone to medical providers or relatives, or when you are talking in hushed tones to your spouse when you think the kids are out of earshot, your children will overhear information about your illness. Sometimes when parents have shared information with their friends or family members, the children of those adults have also heard the news. It is especially hurtful for a child to hear about his parent's illness from another child.

In the absence of straightforward communication from you, your children are likely to end up with misinformation that can create more worry and a feeling of secrecy or mistrust. Overhearing may send the negative message to your children that the illness is too scary to talk about directly with them, or that they are not important enough to be included in the conversation.

For example, an eleven-year-old girl found out about her father's plan to receive specialized medical treatment in another state by overhearing her parents talking about it after they thought she was asleep. The little girl ended up living with the anxiety of what that meant for two weeks until her parents told her that Dad was "going on a trip to visit friends." You can imagine she had plenty of questions by that time, and her parents had to explain that what they said was not true. They also had to work doubly hard over time to convince her that they would always be honest with her about what was going on with her father's illness.

A more serious example is of a sixteen-year-old boy who learned about his mother's cancer recurrence only when he came across the papers for the funeral arrangements that she was making just to be prepared for the worst possibility. He was afraid to ask his parents about it directly and kept his worries to himself. He did, however, have trouble concentrating in school and started staying home rather than going out with his friends as usual. If this boy's parents had talked with him openly about the recurrence, he might have had the opportunity to express his concerns that his mother might die and be reassured about the plans for additional chemotherapy. Although no one could promise that his mother was going to be fine, he might have felt comforted by the shared family experience of concern, the fact that death was not imminent, and knowing that he would be included in important discussions. When his parents eventually told him about the plans for more chemotherapy, he was able to ask specifically about whether she was dying from the disease now and understand that his mother was likely to be able to live with her illness and be treated for some time into the future. This knowledge allowed him to be able to continue to live his own life with as much normalcy as possible during this phase of her illness.

Children will also overhear things from people outside the family, at school or in the media. Encourage them to tell you about these other sources of information so they can check them out with you and have inaccuracies corrected. What a friend's parent says about his experience with ulcerative colitis and the complications he had may have nothing to do with how you'll manage your own colitis and how it will impact your family life.

Talking About a New Diagnosis or a Change in Your Medical Condition

Many parents ask me how to bring up the topic of a new diagnosis or change in medical condition with their children. Any change in health status or ability to do tasks that the child can observe is a good place to start. "You may have noticed that Dad has been more tired recently . . ." "Remember when Mom had that headache and couldn't drive you to soccer practice? She went to the doctor for some tests and found out that she has . . ." If it is possible, you might want to wait until there is a definite diagnosis and treatment plan so that the diagnosis can be presented to the child along with a plan for medical care. This is often reassuring and helps to set the stage for practical planning about maintaining routines. However, if the diagnosis is unclear for an extended period and there is a significant change in the parent's appearance, function, or schedule, children may need to be told that there are ongoing tests to find out what is wrong, and then the doctors will decide how to treat it.

If you have had a longstanding medical condition and there is a more acute change in your diagnosis or treatment plan, children also need to be told so that they do not feel excluded from important family matters. Again, starting with any observable change helps make the change more concrete in children's minds. "It has been hard now that Dad can't get out of bed to play with you anymore. That is because . . ." If the change involves new test results, you can start with "Mom had another CT scan/blood test/doc-tor's appointment this past week, and it showed that . . ."

Seek Out Opportunities to Talk

Most parents have a sense of when their child is most likely to talk openly. For younger children, it may be at bedtime when it is quiet and warm. Older children may be able to toss out a question while you are involved in a routine activity or during a car ride. Especially for emotionally laden questions or discussions, your child may not want to have to look directly at you or have you scrutinizing his or her facial expressions. For example, your child may bring up questions when he or she can turn to look out the car window or focus on the meal you are preparing together. A question from your ten-year-old may not necessarily be an invi-tation to stop what you are doing and sit down in front of him, and doing so may stop the conversation in its tracks. Other times, you may need to pause or offer a reassuring squeeze.

What If You Get Emotional or Upset While Talking About the Illness?

Some parents I have met with wonder whether their emotions or tears might worry their child or make it difficult to talk about the illness. Early in an illness, or when things are not going well, parents may hesitate to talk openly with their children for fear of making things worse or scaring them—especially if your family rarely shows strong emotions. While it is important for you to have other adults with whom you share your biggest fears and worries, you cannot shield your children from your feelings completely. If you do get upset while talking with your kids, acknowledge that you sometimes feel scared, sad, angry, or worried, but that it won't last forever, and let them know it is okay for them to sometimes feel those things too. In fact, sharing a few tears together can reassure children that feelings do not need to be completely overwhelming and that you will be there to support them and try to understand how they feel too.

Think About the Timing of Information

Exactly when to talk with your children about a new diagnosis or change in medical condition may be influenced by other important events in the child or family's life. Some parents hesitate to tell children about an illness before a big test or sports game, or when the child is facing other disappointments or challenges. Decisions to hold off telling your child should be very individual and are sometimes complicated by differences in temperament or schedule for different children in the same family. For example, in one family with two teenage children, one son was preparing for college entrance exams and appreciated that his parents had not told him about his father's new diagnosis of colon cancer until after the exams. His brother, though, wished he had been told immediately and didn't care that he was getting ready to go out of town for a sports tournament. Not getting the information right away made him worry throughout his father's illness that he might not be adequately informed about his dad's condition and medical treatment. Each of these boys wanted to be treated differently, and doing so would have been all right as long as this difference was explicitly discussed with them. Sometimes it is helpful to ask a child how and when he or she wants to receive information. Many older children will express a personal preference and appreciate being included in these decisions. In this case, be sure that the children understand that this might result in their receiving information at different times but that they can always ask to know more at any time.

What If Your Child Refuses to Discuss the Illness?

Many parents worry about the child who has never been much of a talker, the child who says "fine" when you ask how school was or who never seems to ask spontaneously about anything related to the illness. Some children just aren't big talkers, and it is unlikely that they will become one about a parent's illness. Nonetheless, these children deserve to be informed about illness-related issues. They need "news bulletins" and an invitation to ask questions, but parents may need to lower their expectations for discussion. Children, talkers and nontalkers alike, may benefit from being asked periodically if they are hearing too much, too little, or the right amount. Even children who say they don't want to hear anything at all need to receive basic information, especially about things that will directly affect them.

Written Communication Can Be Helpful, Too

For older children, sometimes writing is a useful way to communicate basic information. You want to be sure that there is still room for dialogue and back-and-forth questions, but e-mails or a journal that is kept in a specific place and gets read regularly can be particularly helpful if your child has trouble with strong emotions or wants to receive information on his or her own timetable. A thirteen-year-old girl and her mother would write in a journal about thoughts they had about the progression of the mother's illness, and they would leave it under each other's pillow. These writings would sometimes lead to face-to-face conversations that left both of them feeling closer and less frightened about what was happening. Another family had a teenage boy who wanted "just the facts" and found that e-mail updates and a simple exchange about how his parent's illness would change the family schedule worked well for him.

Welcome and Explore Your Child's Questions

Parents need to welcome all their children's questions warmly. Setting the stage for open questioning will allow your child to feel included and important in the process of dealing with an illness. It will also prevent your child from worrying alone. Answering these questions will often evolve into conversations that can help parents better understand how their children are thinking about the illness, including worries and misconceptions they may have. Such misunderstandings—for example, what caused the disease, whether it is contagious, or what will happen to the parent—create unnecessary anxiety. Conversations with parents can dispel these misconceptions and help children feel that they can talk about even difficult topics.

Sometimes a child's question doesn't seem to make sense, or it raises enormous topics that the parent doesn't know exactly how to address. It can be helpful to try to work out exactly what the child wants to know about. Responding with a question of your own can help clarify this and allow you to address the specific concern. One to try is, "What got you thinking about that?" Children's questions are often simpler or more specific than we realize. "Will Mom be better by summertime?" may not really be about her prognosis but may have behind it the question, "Will we still be able to go on the vacation we had planned?"

When a young child asks, "Where do babies come from?" you probably don't answer with all the anatomical details. Similarly, a question like, "How did Dad get sick?" may not lead to a detailed biological explanation. Sometimes asking the child "How do you think Dad got sick?" can uncover hidden worries or fears that should be addressed. Young children, especially preschoolers, can mistakenly feel responsible for a range of things, including someone else's illness. I have heard kids say things like, "I think Dad got his tumor 'cause I was too rough when we were wrestling" and "I think Mom got sick 'cause I brought a germ home from school." Simple reiterations of how nothing a child does can make a mom or dad get cancer/heart disease/ALS, or specifics about how Mom's illness can't be caught like a cold, can be reassuring.

Questions Don't Always Need Immediate Answers

You might be worried that your child will ask you a question that you can't answer or that you would want to consult someone else about. These may range from medical issues beyond your expertise to larger philosophical or spiritual questions that you would want to discuss with your spouse or clergy. You can still welcome the questions warmly: "That is such a good question, but I need to think about it [or talk with Dad, the doctor, etc.] and get back to you." This does not mean that you can heave a sigh of relief and think you are off the hook, though. You really do need to fig-

Lessons Learned About Communication

- Everyone deserves to know what is going on.
- Euphemisms can be confusing.
- Overhearing something is the worst way to hear it.
- Talk about a new diagnosis or change in your medical condition.
- Seek out opportunities to talk.
- Share your emotions.
- Think about the timing of information.
- Accept some children's unwillingness to talk.
- Communicate in writing when helpful.
- Welcome and explore your child's questions.
- Don't feel pressed to give immediate answers to all questions.
- Help other adults talk with your child about the illness.

ure out what kind of answer to give and present it back to your child at an opportune time.

Communication in Multicultural Households

Some of the joys and challenges of living in a multicultural family can be heightened when a parent is sick. There may be lots of extended family around to care for children, or there may be estrangement from parts of the family. Issues of communication with children are thought of differently in many cultures and may make it difficult to get all the important adults on the same page. Some cultures have more private attitudes about illness in general, and it is considered ill-advised to talk directly about the seriousness of an illness among both adults and children.

If you are living in a family with differences due to marriage across cultures or immigration from another country, you have already faced many of these hurdles. Your children may be being raised very differently from how you were raised. In your family, you may prioritize nonverbal communication over words, or your faith may dictate your beliefs and attitudes about illness. A parent's illness may exacerbate the distinctions between generations or family members and will require all of you to stop and pay attention to what your children seem to need most. It may be that one parent's more expressive approach seems to help the child feel less worried, or that another parent's quiet presence and activity feel most reassuring.

If grandparents challenge the open communication that you have with your children, give them concrete examples of why you think it works best. I worked with a family in which an ill father's mother had come to the United States from her home in an eastern European country to help while he was hospitalized. The grandchildren appreciated her warmth and care, but she did challenge her son and daughter-in-law's style of talking with their middle school–age children about the seriousness of their father's illness and the fact that he might not survive this latest recurrence of cancer. The grandmother also had to face the potential loss of her own son and go through her own anticipatory grief. When the parent-child discussions were placed in the more general context of her grandchildren being raised in a more open American culture, and she could see that they were able to integrate the information and continue with their everyday activities, the grandmother was able to trust her son's judgment and stay engaged in the daily activities of the household.

How to Help Other Adults Talk with Your Child About the Illness

The other adults who interact with your child—teachers, relatives, babysitters, coaches, or parents of your children's friends—may also be in a position to talk with your child about a parent's illness. Ideally, other adult relatives will look to you to set the tone about how to discuss your illness with your children. Sometimes children will go to a trusted aunt or family friend with worries because they are concerned about burdening their parents further. It is important that these significant adults know what language you are using with your children as well as appropriate facts about the illness. They should also know that you are interested in hearing from them about what your child is curious or worried about. (See Chapter 9 for specific ideas about how to include your child's school personnel in the communication loop.)

In thinking about how to talk with your children, it is also important to recognize that especially younger children will naturally talk about what is going on with people outside your home. If you are concerned about privacy or the stigma of certain types of illnesses, be mindful about what your children know and whom they are likely to tell. It is most important, though, to avoid having your children bear the burden of knowing something but being sworn to secrecy.

Older relatives and grandparents may be particularly uncomfortable with an open discussion of illness with children. Sometimes there are generational or cultural ideas about how children should be protected from parental illness, or discomfort with using words like "cancer" or descriptions of bodily functions. Hopefully family members will understand your reasons for being open with your children once you explain that silence and secrecy are most often errors of kindness that lead to further misunderstanding and worry. You might even try having concerned family members read this chapter for themselves.

CHAPTER 6

If Your Child Asks, "Are You Going to Die?"

Many parents with serious illnesses or a new diagnosis say that one of their greatest worries is that their child might ask a question about death. Parents often tell me that the reason they are most reluctant to share any information about their illness or medical condition is the fear that it will lead one of their children to ask about death or imagine it is coming soon. This is especially true for parents with cancer, heart disease, or other illnesses that can shorten life. Some parents want to promise they will never die and others want to dodge the question by saying, "Everyone dies sometime." Neither of these responses engages a child in understanding his or her real worries. It is easy to understand why parents want to say things that at first seem reassuring, but these comments are unlikely to alleviate a child's worries and may increase anxiety by leaving a child alone with questions about a parent's health.

It's hard to offer a good answer to the question, "What do I say if my child asks if I am going to die?" without knowing what illness you are living with and what stage of that illness you are in when your child asks. It is also important to understand your child's stage of development. So what I will do is offer some guiding principles and then give some examples of what a parent might say in a particular medical situation. If death is likely to occur soon (within the next couple of months), you will also want to read Chapter 15 on decisions about end-of-life care.

If your illness is not life-threatening, do not assume that your child knows this. Be sure that when you ask your child about specific worries, you inquire whether he or she is scared that you might die from your illness. This can be an important opportunity to reassure your child about your health. Many children of healthy parents fear the parent will die. They, too, need to have their worries understood and to receive help to establish a sense of security.

Before moving ahead, stop and take stock of what feelings you bring to this discussion with your child. It is not just what your medical team believes about your health status that matters, it is also how you feel yourself. Are you optimistic about the future? Have you found a way to enjoy the present? If you want your child to feel secure now and optimistic about the future, you need to examine your own feelings. Seek emotional support for yourself if you lack the hopefulness and engagement in life that you hope to impart to your children. Sometimes when life is short and time is precious, parents are best able to convey the value of living every minute. Don't assume that if you face a shorter life span or chronic symptoms, it is inevitable to be depressed. Get help. (See the sidebar, "How Are the Adults in the Family Doing?" in Chapter 13 for more on this topic.)

Religious and Spiritual Beliefs

It is hard to answer a child's questions about death without confronting your own beliefs. Whether or not a parent is ill, many children will ask questions about what it means to be "dead" from about age four years. This may be precipitated by another death in the family, the death of a pet at school or at home, or seeing a

Understanding of Death at Different Ages

A child's understanding of death changes with development. Though your child is an individual who may be ahead of or behind his or her peers, the guidelines below outline what children at different ages are likely to understand about death.

- **Infants and toddlers** have no concept of death and so cannot be prepared in advance for a parent's death. After death occurs, a toddler may look in the places associated with the loved parent for many weeks.
- **Preschool-age children** are curious about death. They imagine it is reversible and so think a parent could be dead and later return. At this age it is common for children to imagine their own unrelated actions as the cause of a parent's illness or death; it is important to make sure that the child does not feel to blame for these occurrences.
- **Elementary school–age children (seven to twelve)** understand that death is permanent. They may want to know facts about what happens when organs stop working or why this process cannot be changed by medicine or technology. Many children in this age group imagine they will one day find the cure for their parent's illness.
- **Adolescents** have the capacity to understand death in the same ways that adults do. Their ability to imagine a future without a beloved parent often leads teens to feel very sad imagining what it will be like not to have a parent at graduation, the prom, or their wedding.

All children, especially the youngest ones, will continue to get to know the parent who has died by piecing together the pictures and writings of the parent and the loving stories told by family and friends.

dead bug or animal outside. Your child's questions and curiosity will likely cause you to consider or even reconsider what you believe yourself, what others in the family believe, and what you want to impart to your child.

If you and your child's other parent have a shared set of religious or spiritual beliefs this may be an easier conversation than if you have very divergent viewpoints. Some parents who do not share each other's religious beliefs still can find some comfortable common ground that may include, for example, the belief that the soul exists after the body is no longer functional. Others will need to agree to disagree. These parents may tell their children that since none of us has been dead, there are different opinions about what happens, and then present each of their opinions. Young children are typically comforted by the concept of a loved one in heaven and may gravitate toward this viewpoint. Some older children may reject religious beliefs either as a function of the questioning that is a natural part of development or in response to being angry with a God who allowed a loved parent to become ill. It is nice to be able to share your own religious and spiritual views with your child and then to let your child forge his or her own religious beliefs as he or she grows up. Often these beliefs evolve through childhood and into adulthood. Your child might also be interested in talking with a clergyperson to help place the illness in a religious context and clarify his or her own beliefs.

What Does My Child *Really* Want to Know?

When a child asks, "Are you going to die?" or "Am I going to get what you've got?" he is asking about his own security. He is trying to figure out whether you are healthy enough to be a parent that can be relied upon into the future and if he is safe himself. It is important to feel prepared to answer these common questions, whether you have an illness or are healthy. It is important to provide honest answers that allow your child to feel confident about your trustworthiness in the future and feel that the present is secure and under control. This is achieved by finding a balance that acknowledges that uncertainties exist in the future, but stresses both the stability in the present and what can be counted on as staying the same in the future.

A mother with multiple sclerosis was surprised when she learned that her eleven-year-old son thought she might die while he was away at camp. When she asked him about this worry, he recounted a conversation he had heard in which she said, "Nothing is certain and anything could happen." He knew she had a problem with her brain and thought she could die suddenly like a great aunt who had died of a stroke. Once she learned of his worry and about how it came to be, this mother was able to explain that her neurological symptoms were unpredictable in ways that he had already experienced, that her illness was different from stroke, and that there were many things about her treatment and her symptoms that were already regular for them. For example, when she had a flare-up, she might spend a couple of days in the hospital and receive an intravenous medicine, and his aunt would stay with him at their apartment or he could sleep at his best friend's house. She told him that when he was at camp, she could let the camp director know if she would be going into the hospital, and they could arrange a phone call if he would find that helpful.

If your child asks whether you are going to die, it is essential to understand where the question is coming from at that moment, just as you would explore any other important question your child would ask. You might say something like, "I am glad you shared this with me, and I will give you an honest answer. But first can you tell me if there is something you noticed or heard that got you particularly worried?" Or, "Sometimes kids have a specific worry such as not being able to stay in their house, or go to camp, or go to college—do you have a specific worry like that that you want to ask me about?"

Exploring the worry in more detail helps you understand what your child is thinking about, models for him that it is safe to talk about this with you, and lets him know that it is common to have some particular concerns about the future. Your child may tell you that he or she has no specific worries other than that it would be

Real Life Stories

I am reminded of two children about age twelve, each with a parent living with advanced cancer. One was unprepared for his parent's death, and the other one was anxiously anticipating the parent's death long in advance of the event. The first complained that when he noticed his father's condition worsening, his parents kept denying this and told him repeatedly that his father would not die. Even when he was in a coma in the last days of his life, this child was told that his father would definitely survive. After his father's death, he was angry and felt betrayed. "Everyone knew but me! They lied to me!" he said. He told me that he wished he had been warned that it would take a miracle for his father to survive his cancer and that he had been prepared in the weeks before his father died. He had noticed real changes, and those he trusted told him he was mistaken when he was not. This felt like a lie to him and left him wondering whom he could trust.

The other boy was told that his mother was dying when her cancer was found to be metastatic. Indeed, she had a terminal cancer that was already in many places in her body. Nonetheless, she was still able to walk, talk, eat, and listen to his stories about friends and school. She was actively engaged in the life of their family and socializing with friends. He confided in me that since he had been told that she was "dying," he imagined that every breath she took might be her last and envisioned her falling over dead in the middle of a sentence as they spoke. He felt constantly anxious and sick to his stomach. I was able to talk with him about the way people look at the very end of life when they are dying from cancer and to reassure him that it would be very uncommon for someone to die so abruptly without noticeable changes such as overwhelming fatigue and sleepiness. I was able to tell him that we would let him know when death was very near. He was visibly relieved and thanked me. I am confident he was much better able to enjoy those last months with his mom.

too sad or is simply unthinkable to imagine life without you. As hard as it may be to hear your child's distress and worry, this is a valuable opportunity to talk about hoping for the best, while also expressing confidence in your child's ability to bear even the sadness of your death because of your confidence in her own inner strengths and the knowledge that there are so many other adults who love her and would be there to help her. Many parents will say something like, "My doctors and I are not worried about me dying now, we're focused on treating my [name the specific illness], but if something changes in my medical condition, I promise to tell you. Even though I have no plans to die anytime soon, it might be helpful for you to know all the things that would be the same even if I was gone and who would be here to love you and take care of you."

If you think about it, parents often break life lessons down into manageable pieces for children on an appropriate time line for the event, and this is no different. If your third grader is worrying about living away from home in college, you might inquire about her specific worries, but you would also likely put the timing in context. She does not need to worry about that major transition now. You might suggest that she put that worry on hold for the time being and focus on completing her book report that is due in two days. Similarly, you may tell your child that for now she does not have to worry about you dying, and the best thing you can do for your own health and safety is to continue your treatment and do the routine safety things like wear a seat belt and look both ways crossing the street. If you are not likely to die in the next weeks, your child is best served in the short term by an answer that focuses on reducing her immediate worry.

If Your Progress Is Uncertain

Some illnesses progress in predictable ways, while others do not. It is harder to tell your child that there will be a noticeable change in your health status, for example, before you have another heart attack. Instead, you need to acknowledge that heart attacks can end people's lives, but that you are doing all the things that you know prevent advancing heart disease and increase your chances of living a long time. Let your child know that you feel hopeful about the present and that you aim to enjoy every day as everyone should try to do.

Giving specific examples of how you take care of yourself is helpful, too, such as, "I am taking my cholesterol-lowering medicines, exercising, and staying away from cigarettes." You may need to educate your child about healthy living, including that you can have a rich dessert once in a while without putting yourself at real risk. If you do not talk directly with your child about how you are caring for yourself, he may be left to imagine you are not taking good care of yourself because you do not love him enough to do so.

If It Is Likely That You Will Die Within the Next Few Weeks

If your child asks you or your child's other parent about death at a time when you and your doctors think that you are going to die soon, it is best to ask your child what changes she has noticed in your energy, weight, color, breathing, or other characteristics. If she can name things she has noticed, you can validate her observations. For example, "That's right, I have to wear the oxygen all the time now, and it is still hard for me to walk or even talk for a long time." Let her know that these are the symptoms of the medical condition getting worse and your body getting weaker. Underscore that this has happened in spite of your best efforts and the interventions of your medical team. "The cancer is in so many places in my body now that it is hard for my body parts to work and I won't be able to live too much longer."

Let your child know what you know about how your illness might progress over the next weeks, such as you might get sleepier, need more medicine, or find it harder to talk. Tell him or her what you know, but also what no one can know, and acknowledge how hard the uncertainty is. "It's hard that we don't know how many more days or weeks I have. I am going to keep hoping that I have lots of days and weeks, but I don't think I'll be lucky enough to see the flowers come up this spring [or Christmas arrive or some other specific seasonal or holiday event]." Many children will express disbelief, saying things like, "Who said you are dying? That doctor is stupid and wrong!" Taking a child's hope away is not helpful. So a parent can say something like, "We can keep hoping he is wrong. It feels good to hope for a miracle, but we should also make sure we say everything to each other that needs to be said—in case he is right."

At this time, it is nice to ask a child whether he has regrets or feelings of guilt about things that have gone on between you and him. I can remember a young teenager telling his dying mother that he was sorry he had not kept his room cleaner and had gotten a B+ in math rather than an A. By encouraging him to voice his specific regrets, his mother was able to forgive him and tell him how much she loved his adventurous spirit and loved being his mom. A parent can invite a child to share any anger he feels toward the parent so that they can talk about those feelings, too. Let children know that people who love each other get angry at each other sometimes and that anger does not take away from their true love of each other. Saying good-bye is not as important as a parent telling a child that she is well loved and some of the wonderful reasons why, and letting the child know that the parent is pleased with her and not angry at her for anything.

Guiding Principles

Questions about death should be greeted with the same warm curiosity associated with any question your child asks. Trying to discover the underlying worries will help you address those worries and not leave your child feeling alone with them. Knowing how children understand death at different developmental stages will assist you in exploring for likely worries and addressing them.

Finding a balance between acknowledging that future health is not guaranteed (truthful uncertainty) while providing reassurance about current stability, future supports, and the importance of affirming life in the here and now are important life lessons for all children. If it feels too hard to honestly talk about enjoying the present or believing that the future holds sustaining love and support for your child, it is important to get help for yourself. You need to feel secure yourself to impart that sense of hopefulness to your child.

Different Childhood Coping Styles

A child's consistent style of reacting and coping is referred to as temperament. Children have different temperamental styles. If you have more than one child, you likely can describe real differences in how each of your children reacts to similar situations. One of your children may be very private and rarely share feelings aloud, while another child in your family may be very emotional and tell you about every experience and the intense feelings it has evoked. Two pediatricians, Stella Chess and Alexander Thomas, first described temperament. They studied a group of babies as they grew up and noted that certain aspects of how individual children reacted to the environment were stable and thus somewhat predictable over many years. Some of these factors were general activity level, curiosity or shyness around new situations or new people, attentiveness and persistence with a task, baseline mood, flexibility/adaptability, reaction to how things like clothing or water temperature feel against the skin, and regularity in daily rhythms such as hunger and sleep.

Easy and Difficult Temperaments

Chess and Thomas observed how clusters of these ways of reacting could make a child easy or more difficult to parent. For example, a child with a high activity level, who is uncomfortable with new people and situations, reactive to how things feel against her skin, more often irritable than not, and unhappy transitioning from even a frustrating task on to a different activity would be described as a difficult child. It is important to emphasize that this is not the description of a "bad" child, but rather a child who has a series of reactions to the environment that make it more difficult for her to adapt easily and make her difficult to parent.

Chess and Thomas did not suggest that temperament defined a child in any way that could predict adult functioning, but rather that identifying temperamental style could offer parents a helpful way to understand and support a child's coping style across many years of development. Remember difficult children may be very successful adults. So may easy children and children in the middle zone with some easy reactions and some difficult ones. It is best if you can imagine each of your children as becoming a successful adult. You may find it helpful to think about a successful adult you know who reminds you of your child in certain ways. That person is the proof that your child can grow into a great adult. Your child will feel your sense of ultimate confidence, and it will help your child get there.

Knowing Temperamental Style Helps Parents Anticipate and Plan

By recognizing your child's trademark way of interacting, you can better anticipate his or her probable reaction to the stresses imposed by your medical condition and be more prepared as a parent. For example, there might be days when, because of your doctor's appointments or treatment, you get home at the end of the day after your child's usual bedtime. If you know that your child's daily rhythms are easily disrupted, it's best if you can set up a system that allows him to go to bed on time. One solution might be to get a babysitter or friend to put him to bed at your home before your late-night return. Conversely, if your child falls asleep easily at night and even after a late evening manages fine the next day, you might have her stay with a cousin or friend while you're out and then pick her up after your treatment. Since she doesn't have a strong need for a specific bedtime, the special treat of staying at a cousin's house on a late treatment day may be a great plan. For your child who needs a specific sleep routine, however, late nights at a family member's or friend's house could be a last resort because you know that one evening out would mean difficult bedtimes and a tired and irritable child for the rest of the week.

You Are Already the Expert on Your Child

You know your child best. Together, you have negotiated countless challenges even if your child is still a baby. It is likely that you know far more than you realize about these patterns of coping and how a decision you make on any given day will affect your child's behavior at that moment, later the same day, and for the next day and beyond.

Busy parents often do not take the time to reflect on all the information they have stored up on how each child copes. This is a good time to organize what you already know and keep an eye on what more you can learn. Thinking what plan is most effective not just at a particular moment, but taking into consideration the impact of the solution on your child's coping later that day or the next day, can lead to effectively prioritizing different potential solutions. Using the earlier example, knowing that your child can't tolerate staying up late can lead you to brainstorm the following solutions for nights you have to come home late:

- Get a babysitter who can put him to bed on time.
- Have the treatment on a Friday and let him sleep in the next day.
- Plan a quiet afternoon the next day with an early bedtime.

Recognizing patterns allows the best problem solving to occur.

Ten Questions to Ask Yourself About Your Child's Coping Strategies

Use the answers to these questions to help you come up with a clearer picture of how your child reacts to changes and different situations. This knowledge can help you during this time of changes and uncertainty.

1. How did your baby manage sleeping in different locations, for example, a hotel when you visited another city?
2. How did your child handle the first day of preschool, camp, or first grade?
3. Has every first day been similar, or did your child react differently this year than in the past?
4. How does your child do with an evening babysitter?
5. Does she like all the attention at her birthday parties or not?
6. Does he stay at birthday parties without you, or has she stayed at an overnight?
7. How easily does your child think of a good second choice when his initial request is refused?
8. What things are guaranteed to upset your child?
9. When your child is upset about something, does he tell you or another adult, or is he likely to be silent or aggressive?
10. What accommodations or "tricks" have you learned to decrease your child's distress?

Let Your Child Know You Notice Things That Are Hard for Him or Her

Some first-choice accommodations may not be financially or logistically possible for you. Sometimes no accommodation that you try seems to lessen your child's intense reaction to a particular challenge or disruption. Still, anticipating your child's reaction helps your child anticipate his own reaction, and that may be comforting to him. Again, using the preceding example, you can say something like, "I wish I didn't have to be away until so late. I can tell that it's hard for you when I get back late and you go to sleep so late. It seems like it takes a few days to get yourself back in a good going-to-sleep routine." It is comforting at any age to know that the people who love us are aware of and care about the particular challenges we are facing.

Four Types of Children Who Worry Parents Most

I have found that there are four types of children that parents seem to worry about the most. One is the child who asks lots of questions and seems more focused on the parent's illness than on his own age-appropriate activities and concerns. Another is the child who asks no questions at all but seems to be doing as well as usual at school, with peers, and at home. Still, the parent is not sure what is going on in the head of this very private child. A third child is the rebellious or temperamentally difficult child, who has always been the most distressed child in the family and the most difficult one to soothe. The fourth type of child is a child with developmental disabilities including autism, Asperger's syndrome, or mental retardation. These children always require special accommodation to understand new situations, and a parent's illness and altered routines may be especially difficult for these children to understand.

Tons of Questions and Too Much Focus on Your Illness

Being asked lots of questions is great when, after the questions have been addressed, your child continues to be invested in his daily activities with his usual gusto, for the most part. (If you find questions difficult in general, you'll find pointers on how to deal with questions in a positive way in Chapter 5.) If you usually feel comfortable fielding your child's questions but experience questions about your health very differently, it may be that you wish you did not have to tell your child anything about your medical condition, or you may find his questions make you think about worries of your own. Parenting is always demanding. When you

Five Questions to Ask Yourself

Children are typically less distressed about a parent's illness than most parents imagine. They may react with distress initially, but usually they quickly resume their normal activities. It is okay to show some emotion yourself. It is good modeling for your child to see that sometimes grown-ups can get upset talking about an illness and then resume their usual less emotional, composed state. Talking with your partner, a friend, or a professional about what you do and don't want to say may help you feel ready to field your child's questions. Thinking or talking about these five questions before you talk with your child can also help.

1. What do I think would happen if my child knew I was sick or knew more about my medical condition?
2. Is there something I am afraid to say or something I am afraid to be asked?
3. Am I worried that my child would be too upset to continue in his usual activities if he knew I was ill?
4. Do I feel as if talking about my illness with my child would make it more "real" for me?
5. Am I worried that if my child was upset at the news about my illness and showed her distress that I would get too upset myself and that would be scary for my child?

are ill it is more demanding. You may have some personal work to do to be ready to field your child's questions. Remember that leaving questions unanswered leaves your child alone with her worries, which is not what you want.

If you feel comfortable fielding questions, but after you answer them your child is not soothed and continues to ask question after question, there are a few things you can do to help. One possible source for this problem is that your child has been unable to tell you clearly what he is trying to understand and why, and therefore you have not been able to answer his real question. When this is the case, using the techniques to tease out the real question described in Chapter 5 will usually satisfy your child—at least until a new question arises. If it is your child's usual pattern to ask lots of questions about new situations, it may be a positive sign that your child is coping with your health status in the same way he does other new experiences.

Sometimes, however, a child seems to be so worried about your health that it is interfering with age-appropriate activities and interests. This may or may not be in keeping with this child's usual style of coping. Some children worry about most things, such as starting in a new classroom, trying a new activity, or what others think of her. Teasing out this child's real question may need to be accompanied by the reminder that she was able to deal with the things that seemed overwhelming to her in the past after she had some experience with the new setting, activity, or person. Implicit in this explanation to your child is the reminder that after a troubling start, she met the new challenge. You can let your child know that you expect the changes surrounding your medical condition may be hard for her at first, but you have confidence that as she gets used to the new schedule her worries will fade.

In this situation, it may be helpful to think of yourself as a detective. Sometimes the child with many questions has a specific worry that has not been voiced aloud. If that worry is elicited, the questions drop off for a time and your child talks more about his own activities and interests. Some common things that children worry about include whether you are getting good care, how your illness will affect a specific part of his life, whether he will get your illness, how the family will cope financially with your illness, and whether you will die. (See Chapter 6 for more information on talking about death.)

It may be necessary to offer the child regular times to ask medical questions and then to introduce other topics for discussion, such as your child's studies, athletic events, or friendships, as well as other aspects of your life such as movies you've recently seen,

Worries About the Quality of Your Care

Some children feel like it is their responsibility to keep on top of everything concerning your medical care and find it hard to let the grown-ups be in charge. In this case, it can be helpful to talk about how you and your spouse or other key adults have made sure that you are receiving the best possible care. Remind your child of the professionals helping you with your treatment. It is likely to be helpful if your child sees that you trust your medical caregivers. It may be useful to reflect on whether your child may be hearing you express doubt about your medical plan or the quality of your treatment in discussions with friends or family.

a conversation with a friend, or politics. Showing that you are interested in many topics that are not associated with your illness may help your child turn his focus in other directions as well.

No Questions, but No Signs of Distress

Often parents are surprised by how few questions their children ask. If a child is asking no questions or very few questions, ask yourself whether you have provided well-timed invitations for your child to ask questions and delivered the message that you are comfortable hearing questions and concerns. However, you should know that even when parents provide these opportunities, and have even wished their children would ask more questions, often the questions just do not come.

If your child is not talking with you about your illness but she is preoccupied, anxious, or has had a change in behavior, it is a good idea to think about whom else your child can talk to such as another family member, a friend, or a professional.

But if your child who is asking no questions is also functioning at her usual level in all areas in her life and seems to be doing fine, you may need to accept that this is her best coping style. Some parents imagine that there may be some deep hidden problem, or they believe that children who do not talk much about the illness will have bigger problems arise in the future. If your child reports that he or she is coping well and is functioning well (doing schoolwork, taking part in after-school activities, eating, sleeping, and spending playtime normally), this is not an illusion. Your child may have some worries that are going unexpressed, but this may be because your child does not find talking about your illness helps him or her feel less worried, while engaging in usual activities does.

It is common for parents to tell me that they feel their child is coping remarkably well with the illness in the family, but that neighbors and relatives are telling the parents to be more worried and to seek professional help to uncover hidden distress. Sometimes these people hardly know the child! It is hard to know where this common advice originates, but there is no evidence that "making" a child talk about something helps coping. It is true that adults who faced stresses as children (including parental illness or death) and who felt they were not allowed to talk about the stress and were not included in open communication wish it had been otherwise. However, there is a significant difference

Spouses Need People to Talk with, Too

If you're coparenting with someone who is sick and find yourself wishing your children would talk more about your spouse's illness, it may be a sign that you need another adult to talk with about the illness. It can feel lonely to be a spouse to someone who is ill. You probably have lots of worries that you do not want to burden your partner with. It may seem natural to want to talk to your kids about these difficulties because they are living with your spouse, too, and you may think they can understand where you're coming from. But it is a different experience to have a sick partner as compared to a sick parent. Seek out support for yourself from other adults. In addition to friends and family, be sure to ask your health-care providers about support groups, social workers, or online resources to learn more about what support is available to you.

between the experience of *choosing* not to keep talking about a parent's illness and being *prevented* from asking questions when the child wants to do so.

It is important to share timely information with your child, even if she does not ask for it. Tell her that you want to be sure she hears information about your illness from you instead of by overhearing something. Let her know that you will continue to check in with her from time to time so you know that she is not worrying alone. But ultimately let your child choose whether to talk about your illness with you, with your spouse or another adult, or not at all.

Rebellious or Irritable Children

Your child may have characteristics that make him or her more difficult, or he or she may be in a tough phase of development such as adolescence. He or she may have a history of being inflexible or seeming to overreact to ordinary disappointments. Often parents feel especially guilty about adding the burden of illness-related disruptions to this child's already distressed baseline. At other times this child may be infuriating because she seems so self-absorbed and demanding. She cannot believe that you cannot drive her to the mall late at night, or he storms up to his room after learning that financial stress means he may not be able to get his first choice, brand-name athletic shoes.

Your difficult child may also be your most sensitive child. He or she may especially depend on you as a confidant or as the advocate to run interference in a demanding world. The thought that you may be sick, be unavailable, or even die may seem unbearable to your child. It is your job to remind your difficult child of all the ways she has coped in the past and of all the additional people she has who love her and with whom she can talk.

If your child is a rebellious teenager, often he or she is closer to one parent than the other. If the ill parent is the one your child struggles with most, it is helpful to say aloud that people who love each other are often angry at each other. It is important that your stormy, angry child does not feel guilty about not always liking or being liked by the ill parent. If the opposite is true—the sick parent is the one your child feels closest to and the well parent is seen as the source of most frustrations and misunderstanding—this can be very frightening to the child. Whether your illness is life-threatening or not, your child may be panicky worrying that you may be too sick or even die, leaving her with her non-simpatico parent who will not understand her. When the relationships are very conflicted, it may be helpful to get some family counseling or individual counseling for your child to improve communication. It is always better for a child to feel that both parents understand her, but when the illness could be life-threatening there may not be time for a child to get through a difficult phase in the relationship with the well parent, and professional help is especially timely.

Children Who Have Special Needs

Parents of children with special needs often have particular worries about how their child will be able to understand an illness and deal with the disruptions that come from treatment or limitations in the parent's ability to do things. I am always impressed that parents of special-needs children seem to know their children so well. You may have questions about how to explain your illness or treatment to your child, but I expect that you have already become an expert on the best approaches to explain new things to him or her. Think about how you have explained other changes to your child. What has worked best? What home or school-based supports can be provided to keep routines as consistent as possible?

In general, simple explanation with emphasis on what will be different in your child's day and what will be the same usually has the best results. For example, you might tell your child in advance about changes that might occur in your appearance, and then reinforce the message with an explanation for why you look different. Autistic children are particularly sensitive to changes, whether in your appearance or the daily schedule. If you have the luxury of time to craft a plan, it is helpful to have a small number of caretakers who know your child well. Posting explicit directions for caretakers and being available for consultation if possible is also helpful. Sometimes teachers and after-school counselors can be available to help with caring for your child at key times. Utilize your network both to find support people and to learn successful strategies that other parents have employed or that senior teachers in a special classroom have learned from other families.

The Bottom Line

Past challenges, big and small, are good predictors of how a child will react to a parent's illness. You may see your child nearly exactly in one of the four types of children discussed in this chapter. If your child does not fit one of these temperamental styles, some of the recommendations given may help you think about useful ways to adapt to your child's coping pattern.

I am struck by how much parents worry because their children have never faced a challenge like a parent's illness before and they don't know how their children will react. Little challenges and little solutions are excellent practice for mapping out successful solutions for greater challenges.

You are the expert on your child. Living with the additional stress of your illness means that anticipating and using your parenting expertise to diminish disruption will be important. Plan ahead when you can, and ride out the expectable storm when the inevitable disruptions do happen. Your anticipation can decrease the disruptions and make those that do occur feel less upsetting to your child.

CHAPTER 8

How Your Symptoms Affect Your Children

Different illnesses present different challenges: each has its own set of symptoms and treatment demands. The illness as experienced by your child is as unique as your family. Not every family living with a dad who has diabetes or a mom who had a head injury is the same. Your child's reaction is even more dependent on the limitations the parent is experiencing, including changes in the parent's ability to do particular things, changes in energy level, and what limitations the medical condition may impose on family time and how suddenly or gradually these limitations come on.

These individual characteristics of a medical condition affect how your child feels about your health status. For example, if your child witnessed a medical event that was totally unexpected, such as a first seizure or something that was frightening like an asthma attack necessitating a 911 call, he or she may feel more worried about you than you or your doctors feel. And of course, your child's age and temperament are important factors in how he or she understands and feels about your medical condition.

What can you do to alleviate such concerns? The first thing to do is to communicate openly with your children. (Chapter 5 gives advice on how to do this.) When a child understands that your medical condition is causing a change in your behavior or the rules at home, and that it is not lack of interest in him or her or capriciousness, it is much easier for the child to feel loved and secure within the new family situation. In this chapter, I will give examples of different symptoms caused by common medical conditions. You may want to read even about symptoms that are not particular issues for you because the approach to addressing them may be useful for a different challenge that you do face yourself.

Fatigue

One of the most common symptoms of a serious illness is fatigue. Parenting is an exhausting endeavor even when you have your full energy level, so fatigue is a huge challenge. When healthy, you may have been able to multitask and run from activity to errand and back again. When fatigue is a way of life, you have to be strategic about where you exert your energy. Some people think of their endurance as being like a bank account. There is only so much energy in the bank, and you cannot withdraw and spend what you do not have—or at least not for long. Children from about age five can understand the idea that you have only so much energy each day and that you cannot do everything that they or you might want to do today. Even young children understand the feeling of being tired. That does not mean that children at any age are consistently sympathetic with your limited endurance!

Fatigue does not affect only your physical energy, it also affects emotional energy. When you are tired you are likely to have lower frustration tolerance, a shorter fuse. The mother of a five-year-old shared a typical story about how her fatigue affected her parenting. She had finished cleaning up the play space and gone into the kitchen to clean up there. When she came back into the play area, she found her son had poured out the pieces of a puzzle. He was happily building with blocks alongside the new mess. She felt herself getting furious and she yelled at him. At that moment it felt as if he purposely made a mess to provoke her. In another family, the ill father of a thirteen-year-old girl came home after work and learned that his daughter expected him to take her to the mall to pick up school supplies for the next day. He knew she had been at the mall the day before and had known she would need these school supplies for several days. He could not believe how inconsiderate his daughter seemed to him. He walked out of the room so he would not say something to her that he would later regret as too harsh or out of proportion to her innocent action.

What can you do in a similar situation? First be kind to yourself. You are exhausted. Parenting and managing a household is an endless job. If you can, take three breaths to help yourself feel calmer. Then, focus on damage control. In the first example, the toys that are on the floor are already there, and in the second example, the original trip to the store is over. Yelling about the upsetting situation will not change these facts. It would be best for the mother of the young child to let him know that she does not want him to take out any more toys until he has cleaned up the ones he is using. The parent of the older child might ask her to think about what other supplies she needs before organizing another trip to the mall. Perhaps she can call a friend to see if someone else is going to the mall or has extra supplies, or a neighbor might be asked for help on a day that the parent is feeling particularly tired.

After parents take time to gather their thoughts, it is important to communicate a rule about cleaning up or planning shopping trips that will make sense to the child and will hopefully help avoid this situation in the future. Ultimately, you want your child to feel successful and good about cleanup skills or personal planning. "Cleaning up one puzzle is easy. Cleaning up lots of toys is too hard. The rule of the playroom is only one toy, puzzle, or set of blocks out at one time." "I want you to have the things you need for school, but I want to make as few trips to the stores as possible, and that takes advance planning." Connect the importance of this rule to your diminished energy level. "My chemotherapy medicine makes me really tired. I need you to help me keep the play space cleaned up or the shopping trips to a minimum. I want to spend my energy on doing fun/important things with you."

If, after presenting a consistent set of rules, your child is often not cooperating, rethink the situation. Using the two examples described here, the parent might wonder, "Are there too many toys in the playroom?" or "Do I always take her to the store even when she continues to surprise me with last-minute requests?" Sometimes it's helpful to put the puzzles away in storage for an extended period, or let your child know that you cannot go to the mall at 7 P.M. for colored pencils and she'll just have to share with a friend for a day.

Temporarily losing the chance to do something desirable because of lack of cooperation is an effective way for your child to learn how good behavior benefits her. But remember that this works only if you are consistent about taking away privileges for breaking rules that you've set clearly. Consistent rules and expectations are key when you have to conserve your energy.

Pain

Everything is more difficult when you are in pain, including parenting. Many medical conditions are associated with muscular pain, bone pain, or abdominal pain. Talk to your health-care team to be sure your pain management is as good as it can be. At many larger medical centers, there are specialists in pain control who may be helpful resources.

If your pain is consistent and predictable, making it impossible for you to do things you once did, like lift your child, explain what you can and cannot do to your child. "Since my back surgery, I can't lift you. Luckily, I can snuggle with you on the couch." Telling your child what is possible and being consistent about it will eventually help your child understand the situation, but expect it to take time. How long and how intensely your child resists accepting the rule will depend on her age or temperament. It is helpful for children of all ages to hear that you find your limitations difficult too. You can join your child in the frustration he or she feels, but help direct it against the medical condition and not you. "I really miss being able to pick you up. I wish I never had this back injury."

If your pain is intermittent and sometimes you are better able to engage in certain activities than at other times, this will be harder for your child to understand. It is important to make this aspect explicit. "I know it must be confusing to you. I felt well enough to go swimming last weekend, and today my headache makes it too hard for me to go." Part of what makes intermittent symptoms harder for children is that they have higher expectations of you, and thus feel more disappointed when on one day you cannot do what you did on a previous occasion. Putting this too into words is helpful. "It is really disappointing not being able to go swimming together. It is really hard living with these bad headaches—especially because I can't predict which days I can do lots of fun stuff and which days I can't, and that isn't fair to you."

As you probably already know, being in pain also affects your mood. If you find yourself being short with your children when you are in pain, let them know why: "I am irritable (or grumpy) today. My hands really hurt and it puts me in a bad mood. It isn't your fault." It is key to communicate to your children that the change they notice in your mood is caused not by them but instead by the discomfort you feel in your body.

Sometimes it is not the pain itself but the pain medication that creates the challenge. Pain medication may interfere with your ability to drive a car or even concentrate on the story your child is telling you. Being open about this is important. "I like that my pain medication makes it easier for me to walk, but I don't like that it makes it unsafe for me to drive the car." When pain medication interferes with your level of alertness it is especially important to let your child know that it is the medicine, not your level of interest in his or her story, that leads you to nod off midsentence. "I love hearing about your spelling test at school. I hate that the medicine I am taking makes me fall asleep when I want to be listening!"

However your pain is affecting your actions, mood, or activities, if you let your child know that the pain is the explanation for the change she feels or notices, you protect her from assuming that she has done something bad or thinking that you do not love her enough to give her your full attention or time.

Concentration Problems and Memory Loss

One of the ways to communicate love to children is by listening to them, showing interest in the things that engage and challenge them, and remembering what they have told you. When your illness affects your ability to stay focused on your child's words or activities, it can hurt your child's feelings or make him feel he is unimportant to you. Similarly, if your child tells you about something of importance to him and in a subsequent conversation you have forgotten it, the same unintended emotional injury may occur. Some medical conditions, such as head injuries or brain tumors, may change your previous concentration and memory abilities consistently. Other medical illnesses, like pneumonia with high fever or seizures, may leave you with intermittent changes in your concentration and memory. Still other illnesses may require the use of medications that impair your abilities, as mentioned in the pain section earlier.

It is important to "translate" your behavior to your child so that he can remember that you love him in spite of acting in a way that could seem disinterested. You may be able to explain how your medical condition affects your ability to listen well, or you may need help from another loving adult in your child's life. Your spouse or close friend may be better able to talk about this with your child. "I know how much your dad loves you and is proud of your soccer skill. It is really upsetting when he cannot remember important things, like how you scored that amazing goal on Tuesday! It's really hard that his memory isn't so good since he injured his brain in the car accident."

Give your child permission to have the full range of feelings about frustrating parental inattention, while reminding the child that if the parent were well he would be attentive: "I don't blame you for being mad. You told Mom about your important science test, and she forgot. You need to know that it is because her medicines affect her memory sometimes, not because she doesn't care about how school is going for you."

It may be helpful to write things down on a calendar or in a notebook. These aids can become routine reminders that help you ask your child important follow-up questions. The entries in your notebook may reflect specific things your child has told you about, and your calendar can include important events in your child's school or after-school schedule. "Today was the special assembly. How was it?" "It's Friday. How did you do on the spelling test?" "Are you ready for the game tomorrow against the Hurricanes?" Using these memory aids also offers you the opportunity to explain what you are doing. "I need to write things down more often now. My memory isn't so good and I hate when I forget important things going on in your busy life."

Difficulty Expressing Yourself

Some illnesses are accompanied by difficulty speaking. This may be due to conditions that interfere with your ability to clearly form the words with your mouth or tongue, or those that affect your ability to organize your thoughts into streamlined sentences.

When forming the words is the problem, you may be as frustrated as your child at not being easily understood. Pen and paper, keyboards, or even sign language may be helpful aids. See if you can meet with a speech and language specialist or other members of your medical team to brainstorm about ways to help with this frustrating problem. Remind them that communicating with your children is a priority for you. Remind yourself that often your children value your ability to listen most of all, and that may be easiest for you.

When the problem with expressing yourself originates with your thinking, you may or may not be fully aware of your expressive limitations. You can ask adults you trust to be honest with you about this. Unless you are aware of how slowed your speaking has become, you cannot let your children know that you are aware it is frustrating or confusing to them.

One teenager described his mother's speaking as being like a highway under repair. "It's as if sometimes her thoughts are being rerouted way around so it takes her so long to say what she wants to say, and then other times her words get caught in traffic jams and come out bunched." His mother was very aware of her own struggles to get her thoughts out, so she was able to let him know she understood that it was hard on him, too. He was able to talk with his father about how guilty he felt when he got mad at her for repeating herself or taking so long to say something when he knew she was trying her best. He was comforted when his dad told him that if he was patient most of the time, that was like a B+, which is a great grade for patience, and that he should not hold himself to an A+ standard.

Changes in Appearance

Children of preschool age and older will notice changes in your appearance. Young children may be worried about scars or incisions that look as if they hurt, while bald heads, colostomy bags, diabetes pumps, and other physical changes are often met with enthusiastic curiosity.

Seven- to twelve-year-olds may be self-conscious about a parent not looking like the parents of their friends. Sometimes you can lessen this concern by making accommodations in your appearance such as wearing your wig at your child's athletic games or school performances, but other physical changes such as walking with braces or having one side of your face droop cannot be easily concealed. In these cases, it is important to help your child understand that ultimately participating in her activities is too important to you to let her discomfort keep you away. It may be helpful to see if your child can tell you what he thinks others will be thinking when they see you. Your child may feel better if he knows what words he could use to explain your appearance to his peers. He may decide to prepare his friends in advance of seeing you by using this explanation, or he may feel more relaxed with a plan of what to say if the occasion arises.

Parents—regardless of their appearance—embarrass many adolescents, so it may be difficult to sort out what is normal adolescence and what is a reaction to a change in how you look. It is helpful to ask your child how she feels about it. Welcome the range of feelings she has. Some teens will feel angry at the people who stare at you or who look at you with pity. If you express relative acceptance of your own appearance and a way to understand why people react as they do, you can be a good role model for your child.

Lowered Immunity

Many illnesses and treatments lower your immunity and make it easier for you to get sick with viruses. Concerns about exposure to germs may make it important to enforce strict hand washing in your house and limit friends from visiting, especially those with runny noses. Talk with your health-care team about what is a reasonable level of caution so you do not put yourself at unnecessary risk nor go overboard with restrictions. Talk to the parents of your children's friends; when other adults understand your concern they can call ahead with any information about their own child's health or exposures. A common accommodation at home is to remove shared hand towels from the bathroom and replace them with paper towels that are used once and thrown away.

It is important to clarify that the risk is that you will get sick with a virus, not that you will infect others with your medical condition. It is also important to explain that it is inevitable that you'll get an occasional virus. Otherwise, your child may feel guilty and responsible for this expectable occurrence.

Difficulty Controlling Anger

Medical conditions can lower frustration tolerance for many reasons and make managing anger toward your child difficult. You may be fatigued, on medication, anxious, or have changes in your brain. There is a broad range of degrees to which lowered frustration gets expressed, from minor to dangerous. Some parents feel guilty about getting so angry so fast and recognize it as a change; others have no awareness of the change in their reactions.

Unpredictable and intense outbursts from parents are very frightening to children. Harsh words spoken are difficult to forget. Hitting a child or twisting an arm out of frustration can lead to serious physical and emotional consequences. If you suspect that you are reacting in this way, or if you are sharing parenting with someone who is behaving this way, don't keep it a secret. Talking about it allows accommodations to be made. These may include not participating in frustrating parenting tasks, especially at the end of a tiring day, or not being left alone with young children. It may include using medication or seeking counseling support for the family. No parent wants to hurt his or her children. If you are coparenting with someone who has become explosive, that parent needs to be protected from hurting your children.

Dealing with Other Symptoms

There are many other common symptoms that can change your and your family's lives, such as changes in bowel habits that make it hard to be without a bathroom nearby, inability to eat normally, weakness, dizziness, and loss of vision or hearing. To address any of these symptoms or the many others that you may live with, follow the same basic rules. First understand what is hardest about your symptom from your child's perspective. To do this, you have to ask your child. If there are reasonable ways to decrease the impact of the symptom, seek them out and work on doing them: brainstorm with your medical team and collaborate with your partner, friends, or other caring adults to learn what can be different. Let trusted adults know that the symptom is interfering with your parenting and how.

Then invite your child to be honest about the range of feelings this symptom evokes. Encourage your child to talk with another caring adult about the symptom from her perspective. Your child may worry about hurting your feelings or being misunderstood, which may limit her ability to have a frank discussion with you. It is key to acknowledge the emotional challenge for your child of accepting what cannot be altered, and then to talk about the commitment to being a loving family in spite of the challenge.

CHAPTER 9

Helping the School Support Your Child

School-age children rely on their school to be a home-away-from-home. They have relationships with other adults and children, and school is the environment in which they gain mastery over a range of cognitive, emotional, and physical tasks. It is important for parents to have a good relationship with school staff and communicate about important events that may affect your child at school. A parental illness is no exception. Families certainly have different styles of managing information, and there is a spectrum of ways of handling important family issues from very public to quite private. Each family develops its own ways of addressing these issues with the school, but what is most important is not having a child feel burdened by the secret of a parental illness that affects his or her everyday life.

Pick a Point Person

You may want to choose one staff member to be your point person. This could be the principal or vice-principal, another administrator, a guidance counselor, the school nurse, or your younger child's classroom teacher. Establish a mode of communication that will be easy and accessible. After an initial meeting in person, phone or e-mail updates can be most convenient. Let your child know whom you will be talking with, and find out what ideas your child has to help things go smoothly. Your child may want the staff person to check in with him, or he may just want to know that that person is aware of the family situation if the child feels he needs to talk about your illness. Some children like to have school be an oasis away from the effects of a parent's illness and don't want to have any conversation about the illness at school. This is also quite natural. Many children and teenagers don't want to seem any different from their peers and therefore feel self-conscious when teachers single them out or ask publicly about their parent's health. Talk about these issues with your child first, and then be sure to communicate with your point person what your child wants from him or her.

You can update the point person about changes in the parent's condition or the family schedule, and she can communicate as needed with individual teachers. She can coordinate any special support that your child may need with schoolwork or counseling. You can also let her know that you want to be informed about any changes that are observed in your child's behavior, mood, or academic work so you can respond to these indications of distress. It is important to let the school staff know what language you are using with your child about the illness so they can use words that are familiar to your child.

Many people in the school community will have had their own experiences with illness in the family, and these past experiences may color their reactions to your family's situation and how they interact with your child. Sometimes teachers use their own experience very well to empathize with your child and create a comfortable classroom environment. On the other hand, some people may become overinvolved and intrusive, while others may prefer to be more distant. I knew a child who had been assigned to a classroom teacher because the teacher's father had had the same illness as the student's parent. While some children might

Things to Consider Telling Your School Point Person

- Your diagnosis
- Basic information about your treatment: how long it will last, the side effects, what physical limitations you will have
- What words you use to talk about your illness and your treatment with your child, and what your child's understanding is
- What particular concerns or fears your child has about the illness
- What your child's coping style is, and how he or she asks for help
- Who the other people are in your child's support system
- How you would like to communicate regularly with your point person, and how much the point person can share with other school staff
- How your child wants or doesn't want the point person to check in with him or her directly

Adapted by permission from "Questions: What and How to Ask," Karen Fasciano, Psy.D., When a Parent Has Cancer: Strengthening the School's Response, conference sponsored by The Wellness Community of Greater Boston and Hurricane Voices

find it helpful to know they are not alone in their experience, this teacher sometimes had trouble separating her own experience from this child's, and the child felt uncomfortable with the teacher's sympathetic statements and descriptions of her own past experience. If you feel that your child is not being helped by a particular staff person's approach, you might request a consultation through the school counseling office or an outside mental health professional to help provide some perspective for everyone. Hopefully, school staff will be able to keep the focus on your child's experience and provide support that takes into account the child's individuality and developmental phase.

Sometimes the school nurse becomes someone your child may go to for support, or he or she may play a role in educating other children about the medical problem that is affecting your family. A second-grade girl had been going to the school nurse on a weekly basis complaining of stomachaches and not feeling well. Each time, the nurse couldn't find anything physically wrong, and the child was able to return to her classroom within a few minutes after some reassurance. It turned out that this child's mother had been receiving chemotherapy and had significant bouts of nausea at home afterward. A conversation between this child's parents and the nurse helped the nurse to understand that these physical complaints could be an expression of the child's worry and identification with her mother's symptoms and helped the nurse to reassure this child that she was healthy and able to return to class.

The school nurse might also provide information, along with the classroom teacher, about your illness to your child's class. Be sure that this is something your child feels would be helpful and not make him more self-conscious. Find out what information they will be providing to the class, and have your child preview it, or decide what role she wants to play in the class discussion. For some children it may be important to answer other children's questions and dispel misconceptions about the illness or the effects that it has on individuals and families. You might want to be a guest in the class yourself if your child thinks it would be good to have you there.

The school guidance counselor can also be helpful by either checking in periodically with a child or being available for the child who will initiate contact when he or she is having a hard time or wants to talk. You and the counselor will need to work together with your child to determine how best to provide support that does not feel intrusive or stigmatizing in the presence of classmates. Sometimes counselors provide a "lunch bunch" group meeting with children who are facing similar issues. They can also coordinate a group of the child's choosing: same-age friends and staff members who can provide support and help the child feel less alone with his or her experience.

Keep the Focus on the Child

The school community may reach out to your family in many ways. After hearing about a parental illness, some school personnel want to be helpful by organizing a school event to raise awareness about an illness or having a younger class write "Get well" notes. While these are well-intentioned efforts to support your child, be sure that you discuss them with your child in advance to find out whether they are something he or she wants to participate in. While some children may appreciate the involvement of their peers, others may not like the extra attention to something that is worrisome or makes them feel different. I have met children who have participated in school assemblies talking about their parent's illness, and others who are mortified by having their coach ask about how their dad is feeling after soccer practice.

For younger children who are dropped off or picked up from school, interactions between school staff and parents can be complicated. While the adults may find it a good time to exchange information and updates, a child may feel uncomfortable with the concerned looks or long faces from teachers that accompany an inquiry about a parent's health. Try to keep these everyday routines upbeat, and save any significant or upsetting discussions for an e-mail or phone conversation. It is inevitable, though, that your child will overhear people talking or have adults and peers talk directly with him or her about the illness, so be sure to let your child know that you are interested in what people are saying and can talk with him or her about it.

Check in with Your Child About School Events

Changes in a parent's physical appearance due to illness can also present challenges at school. One third-grade boy talked about feeling embarrassed the first time his father came to pick him up after he had surgery and had to use a cane, feeling that it wasn't his "same dad." After talking with his parents about all the changes surrounding his father's illness and becoming accustomed to what

135

his father was still able to do with him, this boy eventually became less self-conscious about his dad's appearance at school.

If your illness affects your energy and you are able to have only limited participation in your child's school activities, talk with your child about which events are most important for you to attend, and find out what kinds of accommodations might be available if you need them. If there are things that might make it easier for your child, like wearing a cap or wig if your hair has fallen out or sitting in a particular location if you have mobility limitations, talk about these in advance. If you are unable to do something like attend a school play or sporting event, have someone videotape it so that the family can sit together to watch the tape afterward.

Especially for school-age children, the reactions of their classmates to a parent's changed appearance or absence from school events can make them feel self-conscious or embarrassed. Be on alert for reports of teasing or thoughtless questions or comments from other children, and talk with your child about them. Explain that sometimes other children don't understand what is happening with an illness or don't know what to say in an awkward situation. Help your child to find a few simple words to explain or divert attention: "His medicine makes his hair fall out, but it will grow back later." "My mom isn't feeling well, so my aunt came to the play instead." "I don't feel like talking about my dad's illness right now; let's go back to the game." You can also ask your child who at school might be helpful in mediating the responses of other children and supporting your child when he or she needs it. Younger children may need their teacher to address issues directly with the other children or their parents.

Adjust Expectations for Schoolwork When Necessary

Many children will keep school very separate from what is going on at home and will not have any changes in their school performance. It is not uncommon, though, for some children to feel distracted or get lower grades after a parent becomes ill. Sometimes it is the disruption in regular family routines that makes it difficult to have regular homework time or get help from the parent who usually helps with schoolwork. You might consider enlisting a babysitter or other adult to sit with your child during homework time if parents are unavailable. If children will be somewhere other than home in the afternoons or evenings, be sure they have the supplies they need and a quiet place to work.

Other times, a child's worry about the illness can make it hard to concentrate on learning and can affect school performance. After a new diagnosis of an illness, adults talk with me about being distracted at work or having trouble organizing everyday tasks. Children too can have worries and sad feelings that get in the way of school. Often, the change at school is a temporary response to changes in routine or an acute event like surgery or a hospitalization. Children may have trouble doing schoolwork or even want to stay home from school. I knew a fourth grader who had trouble going to school whenever her mother had to go into the hospital. She cried and wanted to stay home with her grandmother and visit her mother during the school day. Her mom gave the child one of her own necklaces to wear to school and arranged for after-school visits to the hospital several times a week, along with daily good-night phone calls. She also alerted the school staff about these plans and arranged for her daughter to have a little extra help from the teacher with a project. If you notice changes in your child's interest in school or ability to do schoolwork, let the school staff know about it so that arrangements can be made for your child to receive help with schoolwork or to make up work later.

If the change lasts for more than four to six weeks, you need to work with the school to provide extra support so your child doesn't fall significantly behind. Talking with a school guidance counselor and the administration about the family stress will allow them to make plans with your child's teachers for extra tutoring or accommodations in deadlines. Be sure to check in with your child about these plans. He may need help adjusting to the extra attention and managing how public or private to be about what is going on at home and why he is having trouble with schoolwork. Nonetheless, it is important for your child to continue to meet some expectations at school so that he is able to maintain a sense of normalcy and competence. Having all the rules go out the window can contribute to a feeling that what is happening with a parent's illness is too terrible to bear and that no one expects him to be able to cope with it.

Find Out About Your Child's Curriculum

Many schools have significant health or science modules devoted to various illnesses. Check with your child's teachers about the curriculum so that you can discuss your family's situation directly with them, and talk with your child about his or her participation. A third-grade girl whose father was very ill in the hospital decided that she didn't want to be in the class in which they discussed the illness her father had, but that she did want to be in the class in which they talked about the different internal organs. In fact, she volunteered to be the child who wore the shirt with all the organs drawn on it to demonstrate where they were inside the body.

Literature can also be a source of learning or possibly distress for your child at school. Children's literature often contains themes of adversity or loss that can help children feel less alone in their experience of a parent's illness. You might ask your child's teacher about having books like this available among the other classroom books to provide a forum to discuss these issues without directly calling attention to your child's situation. Children also often write creative stories about illness or challenges in the family as a way to express their feelings about them. On the other hand, sometimes children find it hard to read about illness or death if those issues feel too close to home. Pay attention to what your child is learning about, and check in with your child and his or her teachers about how school is going.

CHAPTER 10

Hospital Visits

A child who expresses interest in visiting a parent should be taken seriously. Unless there are extreme logistical obstacles, families should support children of all ages coming to the hospital. You might ask your child about anything in particular he or she is looking for in a visit. Sometimes it is simply that a child misses the parent; other times there may be something about the parent's condition or the hospital environment that the child wants to see for himself.

If you have reservations about a child visiting, try to sort these out with other adults before talking about them with the child. Is there something you worry will upset your child? If you are the ill parent, are you reluctant to have your children see you in a compromised state? There are many things that can be done to help these worries, including asking your children directly, "Dad looks kind of different after his surgery. What do you think it would be like for you to see that?" While there are things that a child should be protected from—see the section "Times When Visits Are Best Avoided" later in this chapter—most children can be supported through hospital visits in ways that make visits more helpful than harmful.

Prepare in Advance

Many of the worries that parents and children have about visits can be alleviated with preparation. Numerous adults have told me they wish someone had prepared them for their first hospital visit to a loved one. You or someone who has seen the parent very recently should explain to the child what it will be like at the hospital: the building, the hallway, the room. Is there a roommate? Is it the intensive care unit? How will Mom or Dad look? What machines will he or she be hooked up to? How different does the parent look than the last time the child saw him or her? What will the child be able to do in the room? How will Mom or Dad be able to interact with the child? About how long will the visit last? What are the alternatives if the child wants to step out of the room?

If the parent's medical condition is serious, you should call ahead to nursing staff to determine what you will find when you walk into the room. If possible, work with the nursing staff so you know the patient's schedule. Plan the visit as well as you can

Hospital Visits

Use the following checklist to prepare for a child's hospital visit as explained in this chapter.

- Any child who wants to visit should be supported in doing so.
- Prepare in advance by letting the child know what the visit will be like.
- Help the child get comfortable during the visit.
- Bring an extra adult who can leave when the child is ready to.
- Debrief after the visit by asking what the visit was like for the child.
- Avoid an agitated or confused parent.
- Address concerns for the child who doesn't want to visit.
- Provide alternatives to visits in person such as making phone calls or sending drawings or notes.

around scheduled procedures, personal grooming, and the administration of medications so that the parent is able to be at his or her best for the visit.

During the Visit

The medical condition of the parent will determine what kind of visit the child may be able to have. Explain anything that is different than you had anticipated with the child. For example, if the parent is sleepy, make sure the child understands why—pain medication, a recent procedure—and that it is not that the parent is not happy to see the child.

Children may need a bit of warm-up time to get comfortable with the environment and their parent's appearance. I have heard of young children pausing at the door, looking at a sedated, bandaged, or swollen parent, and asking, "Is that really Mom?" Other children are eager to touch and lie down with their parent, not seeming to notice the tubes or bandages. Reassurance about what is okay and what is not okay is helpful. "It's okay to hold Mom's hand or give her a kiss, but it's not okay to bounce on the bed, hug her sore rib cage, or yell." A child should never be forced to touch a parent if he or she doesn't want to, but many can be reassured that it is okay, even if the child is hesitant at first.

For prolonged hospitalizations, some children get very comfortable in the hospital and develop routines for doing homework or playing quiet games in the room or lounge. Some larger hospitals have professional staff called child life specialists (who are often borrowed from the pediatric ward) who can work with children during visits, facilitating activities and expression of feelings.

Bring an Extra Supportive Adult

For all but the most routine visits, it is often helpful to bring an additional supportive adult. Young children may need close supervision, distraction, or someone to go with them to the gift shop or lounge. Even older children can use an extra adult to keep

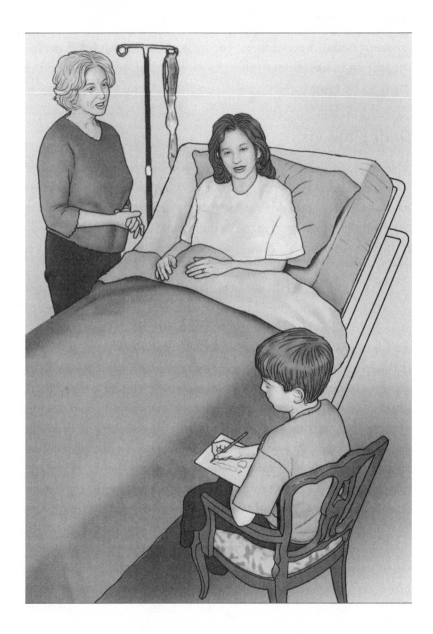

them company elsewhere in the hospital or take them home if they are done visiting but the other parent wants to stay longer.

Be Supportive

In order to make the child as comfortable as possible during a visit and facilitate the next visit, the child needs to feel that whatever he or she was able to do is all right. If the child was only able to stay in the room a few minutes, an adult should acknowledge that even that brief visit meant something to the patient. If the child was wiggly and disruptive, you can make an observation and ask if there is something you can do for next time to make it easier. Certainly give the child lots of positive feedback for anything he or she did well: talking with the ill parent, drawing a picture, sitting quietly when he or she needed to, asking the nurse a question about the IV.

After the Visit

Afterward, find out what the visit was like for the child. What was most surprising? What did she like least? Or best? Was it what she expected? Sometimes the things children notice are the things adults are least likely to notice, and their comments can give you a sense of how they are taking things in. I have heard children be most interested in the roommate who had a special oxygen mask or the person in the elevator who had an amputated leg. Other children are impressed that their parent was more like his or her usual self than they expected, or they found a particular tube or bandage most disturbing. This discussion also helps you plan for the next visit and informs what to consider when the parent comes home.

Times When Visits Are Best Avoided

Occasionally, visits should be postponed or avoided. A parent could be frightening if he is agitated, or alert but unable to recognize the child. If this is a temporary state, it is best to wait until the parent is calm or even sedated for a visit that might not involve a lot of interaction, but at least will not be scary. Children can sometimes sit with a sedated or comatose parent, hold a hand or say a few words, and feel that their parent knows they are there. As described earlier, children can manage many situations if they are well prepared and supported.

When a Child Doesn't Want to Visit

Some children say that they don't want to visit their parent in the hospital. You need to ask the question, "How come?" Younger children may be frightened of what might happen there: that their mom might get a shot, or they might see blood. Specific fears can be addressed directly, "Mom doesn't have to get an injection or have a procedure during your visit. We can always step out of the room if there is something you don't want to see that needs to happen." "There are always nurses and doctors to help out if something happens."

Older children may not want to see their parent looking very ill, or they may just be uncomfortable in a hospital environment. Talking through some of these general worries can help a child to go if you think it is important for a child to visit. You can't force a child to visit, however. You could ask the child, without being judgmental, how the child would feel if he or she doesn't visit, and provide alternatives to in-person visits as described in the next section.

Alternatives to a Visit in Person

Sometimes a visit is just not possible. Phone calls are good alternatives, and modern technology can even allow for video, e-mail, or photo communication. Being able to send a drawing or note and receiving feedback about how much the hospitalized parent appreciated it often feels gratifying to younger children. Many children who aren't able to visit will ask adult visitors how their parent is doing and appreciate some kind of detail about the day or what their parent did at the hospital. For example, "Mom's breathing was a bit better today, and she was able to get up and walk out in the hallway," or "Dad had that tube taken out of his nose today, and he should be able to try eating tomorrow." Even not so happy news can be delivered to keep children included: "That medicine isn't working quite right for Dad's infection, but the doctors are changing to another one that they think will work better."

Visits at the End of Life

If the parent is very ill and not likely to survive, you should make it possible for the child to go for a last visit. Like adults, children and especially teenagers may have things they want to say or hear before someone dies, even if the parent is unconscious. Sometimes children refuse to go for visits when they are worried about the parent dying imminently. You can inquire as described earlier what the child is frightened about and alleviate any specific fears. Sometimes children worry that the parent will die while they are there, and they don't want to see that. You can talk together about how likely that would be and create a plan to support the child through that if necessary. If it is clear that the child or teenager has thought her decision through and can articulate why she doesn't want to visit and that she will feel best about not going, you need to be prepared to support the child's decision not to go even if you disagree. I have had adolescents be very clear that they don't want to visit at the end of life, preferring to remember their parent as they were, and they have felt good about their decision. (See Chapter 15 for more information about end-of-life visits.)

Visits to the hospital can be opportunities to help children understand the illness and feel included in the family experience. Advance preparation, extra support, and conversation afterward can reduce anxiety and provide a shared understanding of the hospital experience. These discussions can soften unpredictable aspects of the visits or children's reaction to them, and they can help everyone to feel more comfortable.

CHAPTER 11

Financial and Legal Considerations

Every family should attend to financial and legal planning, and when you are living with a medical condition this is even more important. It's not easy to think about, but your family will be more secure if you take time to do this. Your illness may affect the length of your life, your ability to work, or your need for additional help at home. It may create additional expenses in medication or treatment costs or in expenses associated with travel to medical care sites.

Because of this, it is more important than ever to know what your financial resources are and how you are currently using them. This is equally true whether you are on a very limited income or have a substantial estate. There are also legal considerations pertaining to the custody of your children if you are unable to care for them, as well as how any money or property you may leave behind for them is managed. Attending to these legal matters in advance protects your children from additional pain and confusion should you die or become incapacitated for any reason, including a truly unforeseen accident that could afflict anyone.

When a parent is ill, children may feel that life is less certain or less secure. Being prepared to answer any questions they have about the "what ifs" such as "Who would I live with?" or "Would we still be able to live in our home?" or "Would I still be able to go to college?" will help your child feel reassured that you are committed to his or her safety and security no matter what happens. This is a loving message. Parents are often surprised that their children have specific worries about the future when the parents have assumed that their children have not considered the "what ifs." Some parents may be concerned that addressing these scenarios may upset the child. My experience is that when asked, many children will reveal these unspoken worries and parents can feel good about being able to address them directly.

Don't Put Off Financial and Legal Planning

For many of us, the tasks associated with financial and legal planning stir up unpleasant thoughts, and so the work of getting organized for the future gets placed on a back burner. When you are living with a medical illness, sometimes addressing these considerations can feel as if it is tempting fate. Often I hear, "I can't even think about those possibilities" or "It's bad luck to shop for a cemetery plot." It is a common coping strategy not to think about what is scary or upsetting, but it is not a good one when you are a parent. It is hard, but it is a very important part of your job as a parent to address future planning now.

Think about writing a will, choosing a guardian for your child, or planning a modified budget like carrying an umbrella just in case it rains. Many of us feel that by carrying an umbrella we prevent the rain from coming. Of course this isn't true, but planning for a rainy day can reduce nagging worries and make it easier for you to respond honestly to your child's questions about the future, should they arise. Hard things are harder when you do them alone. This is a good task to do with your spouse, a good friend who is really organized, or a professional. Sometimes it is that other person who knows you and your family well that can challenge a plan that has some problems. For example, a parent might want to assume that her ex-husband would allow her children to live with her sister and attend their current schools, but her friend may remind her that he has not agreed with other recommendations she has made in the past. It helps to let your family member or friend know that you want to hear his or her honest thoughts about your planning. It does not help you or your children if this person protects you by not challenging a plan that may not work. Once you have done the difficult work of drawing up important documents such as a will, health-care proxy, power of attorney, and living will, make sure the key people know where to find them. Too often these papers have been safely stored in an unknown location.

After reading this section, you may realize that you need professional assistance or that you need a family member or friend willing to be the point person for money issues or for custody concerns. You may want to call on someone else to do the research to find out what makes the most sense for your family's particular needs, or to understand and organize your existing financial affairs. It does not have to be you who tackles all of these tasks, but it does need to be someone you trust.

Your Expenses: What Are You Spending Now?

A good place to start is by assessing your current expenses. Look at the monthly expenses such as rent or mortgage, utility bills, cable costs, car payments, child care, and so on. Then add in expenses like groceries and clothing costs, which you will need to estimate on the average over the year. Remember to include yearly or quarterly expenses such as school tuition or insurance payments. Your credit card company may organize charges on your credit card and provide you with a summary at the end of the year. If you pay for a lot of things with your card, this can be a helpful way to see what you spent in different categories last year.

Don't forget to set aside money for the unpredictable expenses such as car and house repairs and uncovered medical expenses. It's better to guess at what these potential costs may be than to ignore them. Think about where your spending cash goes, too. It is often amazing how much money goes to coffee, fast-food meals, or parking in a week. Don't forget to include the fun stuff such as eating out, going to a movie, purchasing birthday and holiday gifts, or taking a vacation. Sometimes parents worry so much about their finances that they unnecessarily cut back on the fun stuff. It may be that by packing a bag lunch for the days spent at the hospital by visiting family members, money can be redirected to a guilt-free monthly pancake breakfast out with the whole family.

Using this information, put together a monthly and yearly budget. Expect your first attempt at this to overlook some expenses. Think of your budget as a work in progress. There are many resources to help you with this including books, computer programs, and Web-based supports. Check on the Internet or at a bookstore, or see the Resources section at the end of this book. You can use the budget worksheet in Figure 11.1 to help you figure expenses.

Your Income: What's Coming In?

After you determine what's going out, look at the sources of income. Compare your current earnings (and those of your partner, if you have one) after taxes and child support or alimony, if they apply, with your expense list. How are you doing? Are you able to save, or are you currently spending more than you earn? Are there areas in which you think you are overspending that could be trimmed to create a rainy day fund? Do you have savings or assets that you could sell if need be? Some parents assume financial support would be available from extended family members, especially those who have considerable wealth. It is important to talk openly with relatives about these difficult financial matters. In my experience, it is better not to make assumptions because they can lead to resentment and disappointment and can sometimes disrupt family relationships forever. This is hard for everyone, especially your children.

FIGURE 11.1 Budget Worksheet

	Jan.	Feb.	March	April	May	June	July	August	Sept.	Oct.	Nov.	Dec.
Expenses												
Housing—regular (Rent, mortgage, insurance)												
Housing—variable (Repairs, renovation)												
Utilities (Gas, electric, heating oil, phone)												
Insurance (Life, disability, medical)												
Taxes												
Car—regular (Payments, insurance)												
Car—variable (Gas, repairs)												
Medical (Copays, medication, parking, child care, lost wages)												
Food (Groceries, meals out)												
Clothing												

continued

FIGURE 11.1 Budget Worksheet, *continued*

	Jan.	Feb.	March	April	May	June	July	August	Sept.	Oct.	Nov.	Dec.
Expenses												
Household items (Furniture, appliances, decor)												
Entertainment (Movies, vacations, gifts)												
Education (School, college, books)												
Child care (Monthly, extra babysitting)												
Other												
Income												
Salary—regular												
Salary—variable												
Insurance payments (SSI, SSDI, disability/pension)												
Investment income												
Other (Alimony, child support)												

Financial Planning for the Future

You can work on creating a financial plan for a disability scenario and a different one for a death. If you are a two-parent family, do not forget to consider scenarios that include either parent becoming disabled or dying. If you are a blended family, take this into consideration, too. When children in the same family do not all have the same two parents, they are likely being supported with different child support resources. The disability or death of a parent may affect them differently.

Some questions to ask yourself include, Do you have disability insurance? What would it pay were you to become disabled? Some policies pay you in taxable income and some do not. This affects the amount of money that would be available to you each month. Do you have life insurance, and how much would this pay and to whom? Most employers have someone at the company who can help you understand your benefits package. What would the cost be of replacing unpaid work in your family? For example, if you do most of the child care and suddenly could no longer do so, could your spouse continue to work, or would he or she have to cut back or pay for additional child care?

You may be entitled to Social Security (SSI) payments if one parent dies and there are children under eighteen years of age. You may also be entitled to Social Security disability insurance (SSDI). It would be useful to find out what the value of these monthly payments would be and how to file for them should you need to do so. An easy way to better understand these benefits is to go to the Social Security website, socialsecurity.gov. You will find information about disability insurance and survivor benefits at this site, as well as the toll-free number to call for more information.

If you are part of a two-parent family, you'll need to discuss how assets should be allocated should you both pass away. What should be divided equally among the children and what allocated differentially? These are hard conversations to have and difficult decisions to make. Think about the relationships you want to foster among the children and the relationship between the children and the surviving parent or stepparent. Try to make choices that are not divisive or confusing.

I have often seen relationships that were close become disrupted after a parent died because money matters were not discussed explicitly before the death. This is especially true if there is a family business or shared property among members of the deceased parent's family. If there is eventually a remarriage, this can be even more complicated for everyone. Again, if things are not sorted out in life, the children may have problems in family relationships because of the financial strains that occur.

Legal Considerations

There are some decisions that parents can make for their children according to what they believe to be in their children's best interest. There are other decisions that must be guided by what is allowable by law. It is important to be clear about which decisions are yours to make and which will not hold up in a court of law if contested by your children's other family members. It is best to consult a family lawyer in your state to be certain that the provisions you have made for your children in the event of your death or disability are legally sound. This chapter will help outline some key considerations that need to be addressed and documented in writing.

Custody: Whom Will the Children Live With?

This is a complicated question to answer, and it has gotten even more complicated in modern times, when a family is not necessarily made up of two parents and their biological children. But it's critical that you think about this and have a workable plan in place. Here are some ways custody could work in different family scenarios.

When you are married to the other parent of your child and one of you dies, custody will go to the surviving parent. When a married couple agrees on a guardian and includes that person's name in their will, if both parents die the courts will respect their joint choice of a guardian as long as that person is available, willing, and suitable. Extended family members may go to court to ask a judge to change the guardian, but there would have to be a compelling reason for a judge to consider this request, such as the guardian's recent move to a distant location or a change in his or her health status. The extended family members requesting custody would have to make the case that the parent would not have chosen this guardian had the parent known these newer developments. Depending on the age of the child, the judge might seek input from the child to help make an informed decision.

If you are divorced or were never married to your child's other parent, it is a good idea to seek counsel from a family lawyer in your state to learn what the specific laws are that govern your situation. In general, the laws balance parental rights against what is best for the child. Although it varies from state to state and individual judges may give some weight to the best interests of the child, you need to assume that the surviving parent's rights will be the most powerful influence in deciding where your child will live.

Many parents who have been providing the vast majority of the care of their children assume that they can name a guardian in their will and have it be binding. It is easy to argue that our legal system does not make sense, but it remains true that you cannot just pick the person you or your child want to become guardian if there is a surviving parent who may want something different. Stepparents who have not legally adopted their stepchildren do not have parental rights in the eyes of the law. Even if a stepparent has parented your child since early in his life, while his other biological parent has been absent, that well-loved stepparent does not have parental rights.

Some parents have had no contact with the other parent for years. If you have a child who is not an older teenager and it is a reasonable possibility that your illness may shorten your life, it may make sense to contact the absent parent and ask if he or she is willing to voluntarily relinquish parental rights. This would enable your current spouse to adopt your child or make it possible for you to choose a guardian in the event of your death. I give the same advice to people whose children are actively worrying about what would happen if they died—even if the parent is not similarly worried. The court will support a parent relinquishing parental rights to facilitate an adoption by a stepparent. But the court will want to be assured that a child has adequate financial support before discontinuing the biological parent's financial obligation to that child.

Some absentee parents are willing or eager to give up this responsibility and will seize the opportunity to make this transition, especially when it is presented as in the child's best interest. If you're concerned about how to start the conversation, you may want to use something along these lines: "Our daughter wants to know that if anything happens to me, she could live with my sister, whom she knows really well. It would be very hard on her if she had to move to live with you. She does not know you well, and you live in a different place. To provide her this reassurance, I need you to give up your parental rights. If you are willing, I will find out what we need to do to make this legal." Or, "I know you live a full, busy life with your new family there, as I do with mine here. My husband has been doing the daily parenting with our son and would like to adopt him. I hope you will allow it. I think Steven would feel better about this arrangement. We would be responsible for his financial support, and you could continue to send your usual cards and visit when you are in the area."

If the other parent has been abusive in the past, this may help make a case that he or she is unfit to parent. In this case, you may need help from a lawyer. A lawyer can help you understand the specific laws in your state and may recommend that you go to court to seek a guardian ad litem (GAL). A GAL can be assigned to your children to help the judge decide what is in their best interest should you be unable to care for them. The court may decide that a parent is not a safe custodial guardian, and thus the children cannot live with him or with her. This does not necessarily mean that all contact would be severed nor that financial obligations would be discontinued. The parent might be mandated to continue child support but not be permitted to have custody of the children.

How to Find a Lawyer or Financial Planner

You may want to talk with friends and family to get the name of a trusted lawyer with expertise in family law or in estate planning, depending on what you need. Since lawyers usually charge by the hour, you may find that doing some homework on the Internet or reading a book will allow you to focus on key questions. The lawyer will charge you for phone time and his or her research time. Don't be embarrassed to tell the lawyer up front that your goal is to get expert advice and keep the billable time as short as possible. There are some free legal services for individuals who cannot afford legal fees. You can check a local law school or legal aid organization (lsc.gov) for a recommendation.

Friends and family may also be able to provide referrals for a financial planner. Financial planning help may come from someone like a certified public accountant or a lawyer. You can also ask your company's human resources or benefit manager for recommendations. Financial planners will often offer a free introductory visit, so you can include a family member or trusted friend to help you choose someone who will be good for you.

Estate Planning: How Will Money and Property You Leave Provide for Your Children?

If you are able to leave financial resources to help support your children after you die, you want to feel those resources are being used in the best possible way to facilitate a secure environment for your child. The specifics of setting up trusts or other estate planning need to be addressed by a lawyer, but some key considerations are worth noting here. Hopefully, you have confidence in the person who will be your children's guardian. If this is the case, you want that person to be able to use the funds flexibly to take into consideration life events as they unfold and make decisions as he or she thinks you would have. For example, if your child becomes deeply unhappy in high school and there is a private high school that would be much better for her than the public school, you may want her guardian to have the freedom to use some of the college fund to pay tuition at the high school. This requires providing a set of guiding principles for how the funds should be used, but also allowing for the discretion of the guardian.

The guardian of your children and the person or persons who oversee the money in the trust may be different people. This may be because you do not have full confidence in the guardian, for example if the person is your ex-spouse with whom you have had conflicts about child-centered priorities in the past, or this may be because the guardian is warm and loving but not a good money manager or is not the best person to manage a property left to the children.

Even if you have mixed feelings about your children's guardian or the surviving parent with whom they will be living, be careful not to create discord or resentment through the way you allocate resources that will spill over into your child's life. For example, trying to force an unemployed surviving spouse to "finally" get back to work by not allowing him or her access to your life insurance money may cause your children to move from their comfortable home and familiar neighborhood, all in a time when they're grieving. If a family member overseeing the trust fund is left in the position of frustrating the requests of the surviving parent for financial resources that he or she feels are in the children's best interest, this may sour the relationship between the two sides of the family and negatively affect your children's relationship with your parents, siblings, or whoever is overseeing the trust.

Special Considerations for Single or Nonbiological Parents

For children who have a single parent or have nonbiological parents, taking care of legal issues is particularly important. An illness in one parent can highlight the legal status or lack thereof for the other parent. Hospital rules about medical information or visiting being limited to "immediate family" may make hospital stays particularly stressful. A parent without legal guardianship having

One Family's Experience

One family I worked with included a mother who was widowed, her own mother, and a boyfriend who had lived with them and helped care for her two children for several years. Everyone considered the mother's boyfriend the children's other parent, even though the couple was not married and he had not adopted the children. When the mother was hospitalized with complications of diabetes that left her in the intensive care unit for several weeks, her boyfriend had difficulty making arrangements to meet with the ten-year-old and six-year-old children's teachers to create accommodations to their school schedule. During this time, the younger child cut his foot and needed to have stitches at a local emergency room. Since neither the boyfriend nor the grandmother had guardianship to sign the consent forms, they had to explain that the mother was ill and unable to give consent because she was unconscious in the intensive care unit, and they had to convince the health-care providers that they were acting in her stead. Had it been a more serious medical situation for the child, the hospital staff might have been forced to go through a more thorough legal process to designate a temporary guardian who could make medical decisions for the children.

to take over communication with the child's school or pediatrician can raise all kinds of questions. Being clear with health-care providers and school personnel about your parenting role may or may not be enough to get around some of the confidentiality and documentation issues.

Although it is best for all parents to make legal provisions for the care of their children in case they are unable to do so, if you are a single parent or a parent with an estranged spouse whom you would not like to see raise your child, it is particularly important to specifically designate a legal guardian in case you are not able to care for your child. As explained earlier, parents cannot "will" their children to another adult in the event of their death. Just because your current partner has been a functional parent to your children does not mean that your partner will be able to take over their care if he or she doesn't have the legal status to do so. While your written wishes may be taken into account, there are specific guardianship papers that need to be filed, and it is best to consult with a family lawyer to be sure these are in place. If there is another known biological parent, even if this parent is not involved with your children, he or she still has parental legal rights, so you cannot guarantee that the biological parent will not become involved unless there is specific paperwork to ensure that your wishes are upheld.

Why Planning Is So Important

Every family needs to do the financial planning that maximizes security in the event of a parent's disability or death. Every family with children under age eighteen needs a plan for custody or guardianship in the event of a parental death. It often feels emotionally challenging to draw up a real plan with the necessary specific facts and figures. Leaving details about how the family will function in the future vague may feel less scary, but it is not in the best interest of the children. An imperfect plan that acknowledges unwelcome realities, such as a parent with whom the child is not close being the guardian, or financial realities that will limit housing or education choices, may be painful to face. Nonetheless, recognizing these realities allows advance planning such as working on improving the relationship with an estranged parent, considering downsizing current expenses, or exploring scholarship options.

Parents may need a family member, friend, or professional to help them create the best plan for their family. Creating a plan may include researching the laws in your state, going through the family finances with the ill parent who has been the one who attended to financial matters in the past, or creating a new budget. When children know that parents and other caring adults have worked hard to ensure their security in any eventuality, this helps them feel loved and respected. Even when a child does not like the actual options that may face him or her, it is still better for a loving parent to help the child come to terms with these compromises. When this planning has not occurred, children are left alone struggling to adapt to overwhelming or unanticipated situations.

The story of twelve-year-old Martin is a good example of the advantage of talking about future plans. Martin lived with his single mother, Janet, who had advancing kidney disease and was on dialysis. His parents had divorced when he was two. His father, who was married and lived in another state, sent him money at Christmas and on his birthday but otherwise was not in contact with him. When Martin's mother had an infection and was briefly hospitalized, he began talking about his worries. "Who will I live with if you die?" His mother asked him to tell her his specific worries. Martin talked about not really knowing his father and worrying that his father would expect him to come and live with him. He did not want to leave his comfortable neighborhood, his school, and his close friends to live with a father he hardly knew. Janet felt any discussion of guardianship or her death was premature and unnecessary, but Martin was clearly worried. She wanted to reassure Martin that he could live with her mother (his grandmother), who lived in the same town. She was reminded that she could not promise this option without discussing it with Martin's father. Reluctantly, she spoke with Martin's father. He agreed that Martin should continue to live with her family, but to her surprise, he would not agree to her mother being the guardian. Martin's grandmother was in her seventies and had heart disease herself. Martin's father said she was too old. Martin's mother had a family meeting with her four siblings and her mother, all of whom lived in the same community. Her younger brother offered to be Martin's guardian if her health declined. Martin's father felt this was an option he could fully support. Martin was thrilled. Following the family meeting, Martin and his uncle began spending more time together. Fortunately, Janet's health remained stable, and Martin and his uncle forged a closer relationship, which was great for Martin.

The Bottom Line

Financial and legal planning are essential tasks for loving parents. Making sure you understand your legal and financial situation is the first step. Utilize trusted friends and family, and seek professional consultation. Make sure you have completed the necessary documents. Review them with the key adults in your life, and store them in a location that is safe and accessible in an emergency. Following through on this planning may force you to confront difficult potential scenarios in which your child may not have all the financial resources or the emotional support you would ideally wish for. As hard as this might be, you need to help craft the best realistic plan for what may occur. This is one important way to be a loving parent now and into the future.

12

Genetic Testing for Medical Illness: Your Child's Perspective

Many illnesses run in families, and we presume that genes play some role in the transmission of the illness from one generation to the next. However, the state of the science is such that we are able to check only whether a person is carrying a gene predisposing him to some illnesses, not all familial illnesses. For example, adult-onset diabetes may run in your family, but there is not yet a genetic test that can tell us if family members are at risk for the illness until they develop symptoms and are checked for high blood sugar. Some specific types of cancer have genetic tests associated with them, but most do not. If you are worried about an illness running in your family, discuss it with your medical providers to find out if genetic tests are available. Even in the absence of a genetic test, however, being aware that an illness runs in the family can provide opportunities to be vigilant about early signs of the illness or to maintain healthy practices to minimize the likelihood of getting certain kinds of illness. Given the very active development of genetic science, there may be newly emerging diagnostic tests or treatments for diseases that are best detected early. As you will see later in this chapter, though, just because the test is available does not mean that you will necessarily need to have your family members tested.

When to Consider Genetic Testing for Your Children

If the illness that you have carries genetic risk for your children, your doctors can provide information about genetic testing for yourself or your children. Through genetic testing you may learn that you have a gene alteration or alterations that explain your illness and confirm that it is a hereditary condition. Your test results (and your children's other parent's) may be used to determine your children's risk of carrying the genetic alteration—sometimes referred to as "carrying the gene." For some illnesses, if your children carry the gene, they may be at risk for the illness themselves. For other illnesses, they may be able to transmit it to their own children only if they have a child with someone who also has an alteration in the same gene. Other genes are of particular concern only for girls or only for boys because the disease is gender-specific. These are called sex-linked diseases because the gene alterations happen to lie on the same structures in our cells (chromosomes) that also determine a person's gender.

Most genetic testing is done with a blood test, although certain kinds of tests are done on tissue samples that may be taken during surgery or a needle biopsy. It is beyond the scope of this book to discuss all the different kinds of genetic illnesses and tests, but there are a few general principles to consider as you are making decisions about genetic testing.

Principles to Consider

If you have an illness that may involve genetic testing, you will likely meet with a genetic counselor, who is an expert in assessing your risk for a genetic condition and communicating the risks and benefits of testing. However, this individual may or may not be familiar with child development and the emotional impact test results can have on children. Be sure to discuss with the counselor your thoughts about the emotional as well as medical impact of the testing, and explore other resources to support your child if necessary. It is also important to address your own concerns about the impact of the illness or the test results on your family. If you are the parent with the gene, you may feel responsible or guilty about having put your child at risk. If you do not carry the gene, you may need to work hard not to assign blame to the other parent. Try to remember that no one has control over the genes he or she carries, and any of us might carry these genes without knowing it.

In general, testing for children is advisable only when the results will impact their screening tests and treatment. For example, in familial adenomatous polyposis, the child's genetic status determines if he or she needs an annual colonoscopy during childhood to find polyps early and remove them to prevent colon cancer. In the absence of genetic tests results, doctors may recommend annual screening anyway, and so a negative test will actually spare your child the need for screening colonoscopy, which can be experienced as quite invasive. For other illnesses, such as BRCA1 or BRCA2 gene-positive breast cancer, a young woman would not be given a mammogram until she was in her twenties. In this situation, testing during childhood is not useful as there is nothing to be done with the information, and it would serve only to increase anxiety in the family when a child cannot readily process the information.

You also need to be clear about whether having the gene will definitely predict that someone will get the illness, versus a gene that simply puts a person at higher risk for the illness. Although either situation may mean that the child will have medical screening for early signs of the disease, it may feel different to be waiting for the inevitable emergence of the illness as opposed to the idea that one may or may not actually get the disease. These may be questions to ask your health-care providers when considering testing for your children.

It is also important to define your own motivations for having your child tested. Some parents engage in testing due to excessive guilt about having unintentionally put their children at risk for an illness, or in order to try to alleviate their own anxiety even when testing will not clearly benefit their child. Find other adults or medical and genetic professionals to help you sort through these feelings before making a final decision about testing your children. One father I met was feeling so overwhelmed by his own guilt about having an illness that could be transmitted to his children that he could not actively participate in the decision making about having them tested, even though they could be spared invasive screening procedures if the test was negative. A conversation between he and his wife helped him understand that no one else blamed him for this and allowed him to speak more comfortably with his children about the testing and what it was like for him to live with his illness. For some illnesses, there is also the possibility of a parent being tested for a potential genetic component to the illness, even if the child will not be tested immediately. This is particularly useful if the parent may have a shortened life span and the information can be used later to inform medical screening for the child.

How to Talk with Your Child About Testing

If you and your medical providers do feel that it is useful to have your child tested, it is important to prepare your child for the process of testing, a possible meeting with a genetic counselor or doctor, and the results. Your child's developmental level and style of handling information need to be considered. See Chapters 1 and 2 for general overviews of how children understand medical illness and Chapter 5 for more general communication tips.

To start, you need to explore your child's understanding of what the medical illness in your family is, how someone gets it, and the impact it has on people's lives. Young children may not have a sense of the time frame for the development of an illness and may get anxious about their immediate state of health. Even teenagers can be confused by the language of "risk" or "screening" and have misconceptions about how invasive or painful a test may be. You may also need to give children a general sense of what genes are—that genes are the same things that transmit physical or personality traits they have in common with a biological parent. Being able to talk about how genes gave them the same head for numbers as Mom or the same color eyes as Dad can help clarify the idea of a parent having "given" them the genetic predisposition for an illness.

After giving a child an explanation, you can ask, "So if it turns out that you have the gene for this illness, what do you think that would really mean for your health or your life?" You may be surprised at the ideas kids can get, even after having the situation explained to them. Younger children can be very concrete about a parent having "given" them the gene. In addition to addressing your own concerns about this, it may be useful to talk explicitly with them about trying not to assign blame or guilt and to share the experience of feeling that it is unfair and out of one's control.

Adolescents in particular are likely to feel best about the results of testing if they have been clearly informed of the rationale and allowed to participate in the decision about whether or not to be tested. If a child decides he or she does not want to be tested at all, it is important to clarify exactly why and to dispel misconceptions about the results or their impact. If a child or teenager can reasonably articulate her reasons for not wanting to be tested, it may be a good idea to wait a bit and revisit the question later even if you disagree. An exception to this is when there are medical imperatives to test. If, for example, there would be preventive medications or procedures or early treatments that would be done immediately if your child is gene positive, then you should have your medical team thoroughly explain the risks directly to your teenager. A teen that rejects any help at all or has other mental health concerns should be referred for psychological counseling to better understand his or her reasons for refusing a medically necessary test. (See Chapter 13.)

Preparing a child for the process of testing may simply mean talking about a blood test and how long it takes to get the results back. It may also involve preparing the child for meetings with medical personnel and talking with him or her afterward to answer questions the child has about the process. If there are other medical procedures or biopsies involved, you will need to explain those to your child, tell him who can accompany him, and reassure him about what will be done to minimize discomfort or pain.

If Your Child Is Not Biologically Related to You

If you are sick and have an adoptive child or stepchild, you may have particular concerns about threats to your family. Your child may have already survived the loss of not knowing his or her birth parents or another parent who died, and may have developed both resiliency and vulnerability. I have also worked with families in which children were conceived using donor egg or sperm, creating potentially complex family relationships. If your child has always known about his or her parentage and has functioned well socially, he or she is likely to respond to the general approaches recommended for any child and parent with an illness.

If your child does not yet know about his or her biological origins, however, there may be specific issues that come up around a parental illness that is genetic but cannot affect your child. A parental illness may also heighten emotions about relationships and make it feel more urgent to get these issues out into the open. If you have not yet talked with your child about her origins, however, it is important to consider the timing of this discussion relative to the child's developmental level and the other stresses related to a parent's illness. Although many children hear about and integrate their birth stories from very early on in healthy ways, some may not be able to take in this information at the same time that they are processing changes related to an illness in the family. However, you certainly want to avoid having your child inadvertently overhear a discussion about her origins or feel confused about why she is being excluded from genetic testing.

If the Result Is Positive

Parents often dread both hearing the results of genetic testing and, especially if a result is positive, having to talk with their child about it. Again, it should be very clear to everyone before the testing what a positive test will mean about actually getting the disease, increased risk for the illness, and plans for routine medical screening over time. Sometimes medical providers might want to include older children in the appointment at which you receive the results. You will know best whether this is right for your family and your child. If the child is included, make sure medical personnel explain things in language that your child understands, and talk with your child afterward to be sure he or she understood. Often, the adults will get the results alone and be able to discuss them with the child themselves later.

You can explain that the test showed that your child does carry the gene for the illness and what that means both immediately (possibly very little) and in the future. It may be helpful to talk about how while no one is happy that he or she has the gene, knowing means being able to screen for the disease and treat it early or to be better informed about ways to try to keep healthy. If your child asks questions you do not know the answer to, you can reassure him about the importance of the question and let him know you will try to find out the answer from the medical staff and get back to him. This is also another opportunity to have the child repeat back to you what he understands about the results, what they will mean to him, and in what time frame.

If Results Are Different for Siblings

If there is more than one child in the family, you may be faced with having different results for each child. Sex-linked illnesses

169

clearly will affect only one sex or the other, but the unaffected child may still be able to transmit the gene to his or her own offspring of the other sex. If it is not a sex-linked illness and siblings have differing results anyway, there can be a range of emotional reactions. Children can experience feelings of anger at being positive, guilt for being negative, frustration over how unfair it is, worry for the affected sibling, and a changing spectrum of feelings and behaviors. Even before testing you can try to get your child to talk about these feelings by asking, "How would you feel knowing you are negative, but your sister is positive?" or vice versa. Discussing these questions helps children play out different scenarios and normalize some of the expected and understandable feelings. Even though you may be tempted to downplay your child's expressions of anger or envy toward a sibling, your child may need a place to express these and move through them. You can request help from your child's pediatrician or the genetics or subspecialty medical clinic about finding additional emotional support for your child if he or she has a positive test.

Final Reminder

Genetic testing offers much promise in the early treatment and/or prevention of disease. Still, it should be undertaken with attention to the emotional and developmental impact it can have on all members of the family. Often, testing need not be done immediately. It's best to take the time to fully explore the impact of the testing on each family member and to be sure your child is not left with misconceptions or unnecessary worries.

CHAPTER 13

When to Seek Professional Mental Health Services for Your Child

Most children who have an ill parent will adjust relatively well with support from family, school, and friends. However, some children have a more difficult time and can use the support of a professional mental health provider. Parents often ask me how to tell whether or not their child's behavior or emotions are within the expectable range and when they might benefit from more help. Your child's previous experiences and temperament, as well as the level of disruption or distress that your illness causes, will influence this assessment. There are many different kinds of mental health support for children, ranging from school counselors to individual therapists and psychiatrists.

How Much Has Your Child's Behavior Changed Since the Illness?

You are the best judge about whether your child's behavior has changed significantly from before you got sick, and your child's

How Are the Adults in the Family Doing?

Sometimes children's behavior is a reaction to the emotional climate in the household. Certainly the stress of a parental illness can take its toll on your patience with the everyday frustrations of parenting or on your capacity to do more than the bare minimum of household chores. This is true for both the ill parent and the coparent or other caregivers. However, sometimes adult stress can become a more serious problem such as depression or anxiety that will affect your child and make it difficult for you to cope yourself. You may find that you have more days than not of feeling down or depressed or have trouble with your sleep, appetite, or energy above and beyond your medical symptoms. If you have trouble with these and you are not ill, or if you have trouble with lack of motivation or excessive guilt and are not able to enjoy activities you used to enjoy, you should consult with your doctor about treatment for depression. Certainly if you have thoughts that your family would be better off without you, or you have thoughts of hurting yourself, you need to seek professional mental health treatment. You can start with your primary care doctor, who can refer you to a counselor or for further evaluation if you need antidepressant medication. A counselor can also be helpful if you find your anxiety about the illness is interfering with your ability to manage your everyday activities or participate fully in your medical treatment.

personality and coping style prior to the illness may predispose him or her to having more trouble adjusting to your illness. As described in Chapter 7, many parents talk with me about the one child in their family who has always been a bit more prickly, or active, or worried, and the family has found ways to smooth things out so the child's temperament doesn't get in the way of everyday activities. However, sometimes those usual parenting techniques don't work.

For example, a child who has always been anxious and worried may be particularly prone to difficulties adjusting to the illness.

Many anxious children have always been a bit shy or need lots of reassurance about different things. They may be children who had trouble separating from parents for preschool or day care, or who always need to know the plan in advance. They may have other fears or preoccupations and need more support to try something new. If your worried child is asking lots of questions about your illness or needing a little extra attention, but she is reassured by the usual things that soothe her, then she will likely be able to adjust to the illness the way she has with other changes. If, however, your usual methods of supporting her are not helping, or the child's anxieties are interfering with daily activities, then she may need more help. Try to find out what your child is thinking and worrying about—he could have misconceptions that are fueling his fears, and they can be dispelled. If these fears persist and your child is not able to take part in usual activities like going to school, playing with friends, and spending time with family, or if your child develops habits like hand washing, checking light switches, needing to touch things a certain way, or arranging belongings "just so," you should consult with a professional.

Is Your Child Able to Continue to Function in Daily Life?

In general, you need to consider whether your child's behaviors, thoughts, or emotions are interfering with any of the major areas of childhood function: family life, school, and relationships with same-age friends. Many children will have some difficulties in one of these areas during a time of change related to a parent's illness. These difficulties are usually temporary and may require some extra structure or support from adults. For example, during the time of new diagnosis, younger children may have a temporary regression in their sleep habits or be a bit more cranky around everyday transitions. Older children may have trouble concentrating on homework or feel less like going out to play with friends. These changes should be short-lived—no more than a couple of weeks. Extra adult attention for younger kids or help with home-

One Child's Adjustment

An eleven-year-old boy, who was usually an active, outgoing child, had had a little trouble adjusting to his fifth-grade class in a new school. He had been somewhat disruptive in the classroom, testing limits and needing to go to the principal's office once early in the school year. When his father was diagnosed with colon cancer later in the year and was hospitalized for surgery, this boy's grades began to fall. He was sullen and rude to his teacher, despite her trying to reach out to him about his father's illness. In fact, he withdrew further after her questions, getting angry and embarrassed when she tried to talk with him about it in school. He began to pick fights with his friends, and they became less interested in asking him to come out and ride bikes with them after school. At home, he was irritable and had trouble with simple requests and tasks around the house.

His parents became concerned, especially as they knew that the family schedule was going to change when the father started chemotherapy. His parents met with the school guidance counselor, who agreed to meet with this boy once a week. However, the child refused to go to the office with him, not wanting to be singled out from his classmates. The parents consulted with the boy's pediatrician and got a referral to a child psychologist in their area. The psychologist's evaluation found that this boy was likely depressed and could use weekly therapy to work out his feelings about his new school, his worries about his father, and the changes in the family routines. His behavior at school improved after a month or so, and he was able to get back to enjoying activities with his friends and family. He expressed concerns about his father's health and took some time to adjust to the new schedule, but his mood improved overall. The family also consulted with his pediatrician about the possibility of antidepressant medication, but the child improved quickly enough that it was not necessary.

work for older ones should set things back to a certain equilibrium. Sometimes more significant changes in schedule or child-care arrangements need to be made to help your child get back to being able to manage his daily routines and proceed in his own development. (See Chapter 4 for ways to adapt routines if needed.)

If, however, more than one of the three arenas (family, school, and friends) appears to be suffering, the problems persist for more than a few weeks, or they seem to be worsening, you should consider having your child see a mental health professional for assessment and perhaps ongoing support. Any child that has persistent changes in function or has thoughts of self-harm, dangerous behavior, or substance abuse should be referred for mental health evaluation as soon as possible. Be mindful that it can take a while to get an appointment in a child mental health clinic, so err on the side of scheduling something early so that you know support will be in place if you need it.

How to Find a Mental Health Specialist for Your Child

The mental health system can be daunting to navigate for even the most experienced health-care consumer. Just as you would start with your primary care doctor to find your own referral for mental health services, your child's pediatrician can be a good place to start to find a referral for your child. You may be asked about your insurance coverage, as mental health services often have different coverage from general medical services. Your insurance company might have a list of approved mental health providers. In general, you want to be sure that your child sees someone with expertise in children and adolescents, and you might ask specifically about the provider's experience treating a child with a medical illness in the family.

There are many different types of clinicians that can be helpful. Sometimes, a school counselor, social worker, or psychologist is the easiest person to start with. Check with your school administrator or your child's teacher about what services are available in the school and how you can access them. While it is sometimes most convenient to have your child seen by a counselor in school, there may not be enough individual services available, or your child may resist being singled out in front of classmates. Other times, a child may just want to have the school setting be free of reminders of the illness in the family and prefer to see a counselor in the community.

Social workers in community clinics or offices may have experience dealing with families as a whole as well as children individually. Child psychologists may have expertise in cognitive behavioral therapy, other kinds of talking therapy, or neuropsychological testing. Child psychiatrists might do general child or family therapy, as well as be able to prescribe medications for depression or anxiety if necessary. You should be prepared for the clinician to need a few sessions to get to know your child and your family and determine exactly how to help your child over time.

CHAPTER 14

Leaving a Legacy

No matter what people do to stay as healthy as possible, some things are out of their control. A medical condition may shorten a parent's life and thus deprive him or her of the opportunity to see a child grow into adulthood, marry, or become a parent him- or herself. Facing this potential, many parents seek to create a legacy gift for their children that can be enjoyed long after the parent is gone. While these gifts may be designed to help a child to continue to feel a deceased parent's love, these same gifts can also be treasured when shared during a parent's long life.

Think of a legacy as a gift given from one generation to the next. It can be an important belonging, such as a special item of jewelry, a favorite piece of furniture, or a signature clothing item. Legacy gifts can be important communications such as a letter written to a child, a family album, or a meaningful story transcribed into a journal. You may think of them as family traditions, carried on even when parents are not ill. For example, in my family the tradition of passing on special pieces of jewelry has occurred while the giver was alive and well and could enjoy the symbolic sharing of these special items. By sharing a piece of family jewelry this way, the giver is able to tell the stories that give the piece its important meaning. While always special, these symbolic gifts take an even more cherished place after the loved family member who gave it dies. It allows the recipient a symbolic way to remain connected to the beloved person being grieved.

When a loved family member dies, it is common to seek ways to feel that the loved person is included in the ongoing life of the family. Survivors commonly wish that the person who died could approve current life choices or celebrate recent successes. Children often want to know who their parent was as a person. The pursuit of this understanding can be aided by shared stories and meaningful gifts that provide comfort and connection. The process of considering what you might want to share with your children may itself be a great opportunity to talk about which belongings or values of yours you would want each of your children to own or incorporate into his or her later life and why it is important. The conversations about these gifts may be as cherished as the gifts themselves.

Guiding Principles

When you are thinking about intergenerational gifts, be sure to remember and acknowledge each of your children as equally as you are able. Ideally, these gifts promote your child's feeling of being well loved and well known by you, and do not leave one child to feel more or less loved than another. For example, if you decide to write individual letters to your children, be mindful of making each letter about the same length and similarly personalized. It is hard to make a series of gifts exactly equal, but you can tell your children in life or in a letter that this is your intent. For example, "I hope each of you knows how much I love you. I am leaving special things to each of you and hope you will enjoy what you have been given. Whatever their monetary value, each of these things has been special to me and comes with the same amount of my love and the deepest wish that it will bring you new pleasures and good memories."

It is important to try to leave gifts in a way that helps your children pull together, not in a way that pulls them apart. Designating what is for whom may help prevent fighting over who gets which items. If your children are young, you may leave a letter with your will that includes which pieces of jewelry or other valuables you hope will go to them when they are adults. This letter can include a little story about each item and what makes it meaningful.

Letting Your Child Choose Something Personal

Your child may want to choose to keep special things from your current belongings. He or she may choose these when you are nearing the end of your life or may want to pick things with the help of your spouse or another close adult after your death. Often children will choose a familiar item of a parent's clothing such as a hat, scarf, or favorite jacket. They often want to keep that item in their own bedroom and may draw comfort from holding it or wearing it after the parent is gone. Sometimes that article of clothing is one the parent wore in a photo with the child or during a special occasion. Many times it is a frequently worn item of clothing. A close family member can invite your child to share the special meaning of the chosen item. Some children will want to share their personal story about this piece of clothing, and others will choose to keep the meaning of the chosen article private. Either choice is fine.

Existing Family Traditions

In some families, there are already legacy gifts. Perhaps you have your grandmother's candlesticks, your father's cuff links, or a family Bible. As you consider the gifts you might like to leave for your children, begin with those intergenerational gifts that are already part of your family life. These special items can be enjoyed as they are being used and can also present an opportunity for you to tell stories about their original owners or the past events associated with their use. If your children are young, you may want to write down these family stories or get help from family members in documenting their history and meaning.

Examples from Parents

After her pancreatic cancer diagnosis, while one mom was thinking of legacy gifts to leave her children, she talked about a favorite cast-iron skillet of her grandmother's that she used to make Sunday breakfasts. She often told her children stories of childhood visits to her grandmother's house when she used that skillet. Thinking about this special skillet helped her to think of things she used during family times that might bring her children the same happy associations. She began to make her daughters recipe boxes with favorite recipes. She included memories on some of the recipes, such as a funny thing one of the girls said at a meal or where the food was eaten.

A father with ALS talked about the pleasure he felt in knowing that his son wore his deceased grandfather's cuff links at his bar mitzvah. This father felt like his own father was symbolically in attendance at this important event. Though his son was told about the meaning of the cuff links, he was still too young to fully appreciate their intergenerational significance, so his father wrote a letter to his son describing the many feelings he had that day. He hoped his son would one day want to reread this letter when his own son was ready for a bar mitzvah.

Other parents make annotated photo albums for each child with special memories and favorite moments written alongside each photo. It is great to document fun and funny times and to imagine your child's smile or laughter at the memories. These albums become vehicles through which children can almost feel like they are having a wonderful conversation with you.

Your Child's Name as a Legacy

One common legacy that is intangible is the passing on of a name. Different traditions call for this generational acknowledgment to be done differently. Some families may use names that honor the living, while others may honor a relative who has already died.

There are parents who name their children after special places or special people in their lives. If your child's name has a story, make a point of telling her how she got her name. You can talk about all the love and consideration that went into choosing her name as well as what you loved about the person whose name she was given. Naming is a symbol of all the hopes and dreams that went into anticipating your child's welcome to the world. By talking together, she can ask you questions and enrich the storytelling.

Even when you have had this conversation, and especially if your child is younger, it is a great gift to write down the history of your child's name for her to keep and reread. This story may include your reflections on holding your child for the first time or the pleasure and pride you felt when your child was first born. Children of all ages want to know what their parent saw in them that was special and what was wonderful about the experience of parenting them.

Legacy Funds

Sometimes parents will put aside small or larger amounts of money to allow a child to do something special. A parent's illness is expensive, so this may not be possible, but when it is, it can be another way of sharing a tradition. I know one mother who left money for her young son with her sister. She instructed her sister to wait until he was a teenager and then take him shopping and let him choose things for his bedroom. She imagined that maybe he would want to paint his room a new color or buy a trendy lamp or posters. She remembered wishing she could express herself in her room as a teenager and not being able to afford to do so. Another mother left money for her elementary school–age daughter to do something special for herself on prom day. This mother imagined her daughter might want special shoes, a manicure, or to have her hair done for the event. Many parents leave education funds if they can afford to do so, and some leave funds for travel.

Other Ideas for Your Legacy Gift

The examples below may spur you on to put together a similar legacy for your child, or they may spark an idea for a different intergenerational gift:

- **Make a library or book list.** You could list your favorite books from different times in your life and why you loved each of the books. If you own the books, you may want to put inscriptions in them for your child. These books may be the beginnings of your child's own library. Alternatively, you may have favorite books that you read to your child. Pick one or two favorites and tell your child what you loved about reading that book to him at a particular age and why. This could be a special picture book or the first book your child read on his own. You can write a letter to accompany a copy of the special book and put it away for your child. Perhaps she will read the book to your grandchild one day. You can enjoy imagining this possibility whether or not you will have the pleasure of being there when it happens.
- **Put together a music library.** It may be a list of favorite songs or symphonies from different times in your life or may include some actual CDs that are special to you or that remind you of times spent with your child. For example, what lullaby or car music was a regular when your child was younger? If you can make the time to write down what makes each choice special and give as detailed a memory as possible, it will be easiest for your child to feel connected and able to get to know you a little better.
- **Create a must-see movie list.** Include your favorite films and what it was that made them special to you. Like the book or music library, think about the movie selections that were special to you as well as selections that have meaning in your relationship with your child. Having this list will be almost as if he is able to watch the movie with you.

- **Organize your hobby supplies.** Put woodworking tools, fishing tackle, art materials, or other important things together that your child could use in later adolescence or adulthood if he or she chooses to pursue an interest that you have. Include a letter or brief note letting the next generation know what made this interest special for you. Often, your child will want to try this special pursuit at some point in his or her life. If not, the letter and tools or equipment may still be treasured for their special meaning to you.

- **Create a recipe box.** Make recipe cards for favorite family meals and special occasion dishes. Add photos and stories. Do not hesitate to include the funny stories and recipe failures. You can invite extended family to include their favorite recipes too. Eating together is connected to family feelings. Special food with all its aromas and familiar tastes can create a powerful link and tap into important memories.

- **Make a scrapbook.** Ask everyone, including children, to bring a favorite family story to the next holiday or celebration. Put everyone's stories together in a scrapbook. Include photos or a videotape of the event if possible. Creating a family archive is a wonderful gift to the next generation. Often when people are asked what one thing they would save from their home if it were on fire, it is the family photos or videos. They are that special.

- **Make a Web page.** In this age of the Internet, many families use e-mail and Web-based communication. You can create a rich multimedia document on the Web that can include many of your interests, interactions with friends, and musings. If you use this vehicle for expression and connection, consider what parts of your Web page you want to save for your children. It is hard to know what will be accessible from this virtual collection in the future, so it is important to have a way to save your creation to ensure it will be available to your children years from now.

- **Enable your children to meet your old friends.** Make a list of friends or family whom your children can talk to about you as they get older. No one person knows all about any of one of us. There are, no doubt, several people from different times in your life who know parts of your personal story. Often people have lost contact with special people from earlier phases of life, and this can be an opportunity to reconnect with old friends and mentors. Call or write old friends and enjoy catching up while asking them to be on your children's contact list.

- **Pass down religious items.** If religious items such as a family Bible, a prayer book, rosary beads, Friday night candles, or a christening gown have been part of your family traditions, they can be special legacy gifts to your children. Providing your child with her own religious items to use during your life will help these items to be infused with your love and sentiment long after you are gone. Rituals are often very comforting during times of grief, and a well-worn prayer book or set of candlesticks can provide familiarity and a sense of normalcy at a difficult time.

Closing Thoughts

Your child will have an evolving, changing relationship with you even after you have died, whether or not you have an untimely death from your illness. There is no way to anticipate every question that may arise in the future, nor is it possible to create a legacy that circumvents a child's grief at your loss. Still, there are many ways that you can leave gifts to your children that help them appreciate how much you love them and aid them in learning who this incredibly important parent, you, really was. There are many examples of legacies described in this chapter. Don't take this to mean that you have to do each and every one. You may also need significant help from others to create certain kinds of legacies. It is absolutely not the intent of this chapter to overwhelm you. Perhaps pick one thing to write about and one item you envision going to your child. Start simple, and if you enjoy the process you may choose to do more, and if not, you will have left a small but wonderful gift of yourself to each of your children.

CHAPTER 15

Making Decisions About End-of-Life Care

If treatment for your illness is no longer possible and it is continuing to get worse, the focus of your care may shift to making you as comfortable and functional as you can be at the end of life. At this point, your medical providers may talk with you about receiving hospice or palliative care. Depending on the resources in your area, you may be able to choose to receive end-of-life care at home, in an inpatient hospice, or in an acute care hospital. Your preferences may depend on many things, including practical considerations, past experiences with hospice or others' deaths, your own personal wishes about where you want to die, and your children's views. As difficult as it is to think about and plan for the end of one's life, it is best for your children if you plan for this eventuality so their needs can be addressed as thoughtfully as possible. You may be reading this chapter as the caregiver for someone nearing the end of life. Many of the following decisions may fall to you during a very difficult time for yourself. Having some discussions with your ill partner as he or she is able may help you feel more comfortable about later making these decisions on your own if you need to.

How to Decide Where a Parent Will Be at the End of Life

In some families, the wishes of the ill parent will be the sole factor that determines where he or she will receive end-of-life care. For others, there are many other considerations, including distance between home and the hospice center, the availability of appropriate space in the home, or the feelings of particular family members about having the parent be cared for and die at home. It is important to communicate about the different perspectives within your family and be able to come to some common decisions. Children should be given opportunities to participate in some of these discussions and express their own fears, worries, and possible misconceptions so that they can be addressed.

If a Parent Will Be Cared for in a Residential or Inpatient Hospice

If you decide to receive end-of-life care in an inpatient setting such as a hospice or acute care hospital, you will need to consider how and when different family members will be able to visit and spend quality time. Spouses, coparents, and grandparents have to manage many competing responsibilities that complicate the medical care of a parent with a terminal illness. While many partners want to constantly be at their loved one's hospital bedside, they may feel torn by the needs of children at home. If familiar and loving adults can care for children, however, they will better be able to manage the absence of both the ill and the well parent.

If children will be visiting, they may need help preparing for the hospice environment and the physical changes in their parent's appearance and function, as well as help with how best to spend their time during a visit. (See Chapter 10 for more general ideas about how to manage hospital visits with children.) If a parent is very sleepy or comatose, children may need guidance and supplies for quiet activities to do while the family is visiting. It is also useful to have extra adults to take the child outside or home early if

Different Choices

There are as many different ways to manage the end of life as there are family styles. I have seen children and adults alike cope well with a wide range of choices, especially when there is forethought and open discussion about how to handle things.

I worked with one family in which a mom was very clear that she did not want to be cared for at home. She had taken care of her own mother at the end of her life and did not want to burden her family with that experience. She arranged in advance to be transferred to the hospital when her pain made it difficult for her to manage at home. Her husband and children were able to drive in daily to see her, and the children had close relatives to stay at home with them when their father needed to stay at the hospital longer.

On the other hand, I have cared for several families in which a parent very much wanted to die in his or her own home and the family members were happy to provide company and care during the last days. These parents' children were involved and well cared for by the many loving adults who came to spend time and help out. They were able to be comfortable in their own home and decide for themselves how much time to spend at the parent's bedside.

I have also had the opportunity to talk with the family of a patient named Debbie about her wish to die at home. The father and teenage daughter were both concerned about whether Debbie could receive the right care at home, and they didn't want to see her uncomfortable. In addition, they were both very worried about how it would feel to them if she died in their home. The daughter in particular wondered if she would find it too difficult to live in the same house afterward. Even though they worried about hurting Debbie by not agreeing easily to her wish to receive hospice at home, they decided to talk about their concerns with her. Ultimately, Debbie and her family decided that a hospice center in their community would be able to provide the care Debbie hoped for and would allow frequent visits without making anyone in the family too uncomfortable.

the child is done visiting but other family members want to stay. Hospices may also have special staff to provide social support for adults and age-appropriate activities and information for children.

If a Parent Will Be Cared for at Home

Sometimes having home hospice care is the best way for the well parent to be available to both the ill spouse and their children. If this seems right for your family, be sure that you understand how specific medical and physical needs will be met. Being confident that you have whatever medical care you need available will make sure that not only your needs but also your children's are met. Some people that I talk with are most worried about who will take physical care of the ill parent. Will twenty-four-hour nursing care be required, or can adult family members handle most of the care with guidance and visits from medical staff? Others worry most about pain control and who will administer medications. Will special medical equipment be necessary: oxygen, a wheelchair, a hospital bed, intravenous or tube feedings? Many of these things can readily be provided at home, but you will need to discuss these specifically with the hospice care company that you will be working with. These agencies may also have social services that can attend to the emotional needs of your family at home.

In addition to access to appropriate medical care and equipment, you also need to consider the physical setup in your house. It is best for care to occur in a room with a door so the children can visit with you when they like but can also move about their home without always having to walk through a room with medical equipment or a very ill parent. There may also be a need for privacy for certain medical procedures or routine hygiene. If at all possible, try not to displace your child from spaces in your home that give him or her comfort, whether that be the child's own room or a common family area that he or she spends a lot of time in. If a child's space needs to be disrupted, be sure to acknowledge his or her upset feelings about it and communicate how much you appreciate your child's flexibility.

Families will also make different decisions about whether children will go to school every day during the very last stages of a parent's life. Ask your children about their preferences, and consider who else will be at home to help care for them. You don't want to force a child to go to school if he or she really wants to stay home with the family, but you also don't want to keep your child home for prolonged periods of time without any structure or when he or she cannot be well taken care of.

Discuss How Children Want to Hear About a Parent's Death

Since the dying process may be unpredictable, you should discuss early on how the different members of the family want to be informed about an eventual death. While some illnesses result in a gradual decline and a more predictable sequence of physical symptoms, coma, and death, other illnesses may involve sudden events that lead to death. In either case, the uncertainty is often very difficult to bear. While no one can control exactly how or when someone will die, even children can be given some sense of control over how they hear about it. For example, children who are school-age and older can be asked how they want to be told about a parent's actual death: do they want to be woken up if it happens at night? How about if it happens while they are at school? What do they want to do after they learn about the death?

If it becomes clear that death is coming soon, children can also be given opportunities to say some kind of good-bye. Children's capacities to do this meaningfully will vary, not necessarily by age, but also by their own personality style and general style of communicating with their ill parent. In general, give children specific opportunities to say good-bye without having any expectation that they will either want to or be able to really do so. Some older children may want private time, and many will want the company of a familiar and loving adult to sit with them while they say a last "I love you." There will be subsequent opportunities to say good-bye at memorial services or funerals as well (see Chapter 16).

191

If the death will occur at home, you should also think about where the children will be during that time. There are no right answers about whether or not to include children in these last moments. Like many decisions during illness, this is very personal. I worked with one family in which the young teenagers wanted to be home, but the father felt they should be at their grand-mother's house when their mother died. In the end, that is where they were, but because it had been actively discussed, they were able to feel all right about it even though it wasn't what they orig-inally wanted. If the decision is to have older children or teenag-ers present with other family members, talk together with your hospice care workers about what you can expect at the very end of life and how the ill parent will be made as comfortable as pos-sible. There are often changes in breathing or body temperature that can be anticipated. Be sure your children have specific adults who will be available to them if they want to leave or need addi-tional support. Very young children will not be able to process what is happening and may be more distracting and distressing to have around, or they may be upset by the emotional atmosphere. If possible, they can be cared for by other familiar adults and eventually hear the story when they are older and curious about it.

Also think about where you or your children will be when the medical or coroner's staff comes. This can be distressing for many people, and you may want to make arrangements to have the chil-dren in another area of the house or with other close family or friends during this time. You should be prepared for children to want to know specifics about where the body will go and what arrangements have been made for the wake, funeral, or services. (See Chapter 16 for additional guidance about these events.)

Deciding how to include your children in end-of-life care is never simple. Even if things don't happen as hoped, supportive adults can help children understand that decisions were made thoughtfully and that people who love them will help them man-age their loss over time.

Funerals and Memorial Services

Every culture and religion has traditions surrounding the death of a loved one. Most of these customs bring together the community to recognize and provide comfort to the family at the time of their painful loss. Many will celebrate the meaning of the person's life and voice beliefs about how the spirit or soul exists into the future after the body has failed. There are many different religious and secular traditions for funerals and memorial services. When possible, a person shares with loved ones his or her own wishes for these services while alive, incorporates the wishes of the survivors, and allows the planning for the funeral or memorial service to begin before death. Some families have a strong religious or cultural tradition that provides the basic structure for the funeral, others have a mix of cultural traditions that may mesh or be in conflict with each other, and still others have no traditions to incorporate. It is a gift to the survivors to let them know what you would want so that they can feel that they are authentically honoring you in this last life ceremony.

Family Conflict Makes Planning Harder

When family relationships are conflicted in life, it may be difficult to plan a funeral or memorial service that satisfies everyone.

By talking openly about funeral wishes, some areas of conflict between parents, partners, and siblings may be uncovered, such as which religious tradition to follow, who will preside, or where the funeral will occur. It is better to sort out these conflicts before death rather than having them negatively affect the family and extended family relationships after one's death.

Making Your Child's Needs the Priority

Making the needs of your child a priority can be a helpful way to make your final decisions about funeral plans. For example, consider having the presiding person be someone your child knows, having a ceremony in a setting that is familiar to your child or permits your child's friends to be in attendance, and having the burial site or ashes in a location that your child can visit relatively easily. The most important aspect of the funeral preparation is making sure a close adult talks with your child in advance about what he or she will see and talks with your child afterward about what he or she saw and felt. These conversations usually occur after the loved person has died or in the last days of his or her life.

In order to be able to prepare your child for the funeral, your coparent or another loving adult has to be prepared to explain the details of the funeral process to your child. The adult should talk with the clergyperson who will preside, funeral home personnel, and the cemetery director or director at the cremation facility and ask each of them the kind of specific questions your child might ask. The adult will need to know how to reach each of these people after these initial conversations so that he or she can get the answers to any additional unanticipated questions your child asks. The adult helper may want to begin this process before the death occurs, even though the detailed discussion with your child usually occurs after the death has happened. The exception to this time schedule is when a child comes to a parent or other relative asking questions in advance. For this child, it is important to understand the origin of the question or questions and then to find good answers to them, whenever the questions arise.

How Young Is Too Young?

Most children will attend a funeral or memorial service for a parent from about age four onward. A parent may choose not to bring the youngest children to the cemetery, especially if the coffin will be lowered into the ground at the end of the graveside ceremony. The reason for this is concern about the child watching the coffin go into the ground and perhaps worrying that the parent is in a cold place or even being put in the ground without really being dead. It is useful to tell a child who is not going to the graveside what will happen at the cemetery and let her know that in the future she will visit the cemetery together with the surviving parent or another loved family member. If a child protests being excluded from the portion of the service that occurs at the cemetery, it is probably best to include her regardless of age.

It is important for young children to be assigned a caring, familiar adult to accompany them throughout the ceremony. This person should be told to leave the ceremony if the child becomes restless or overly distressed. The adults in the immediate family will usually want to be present for the entire service, so the adult designated to accompany the child needs to be someone who will be comfortable missing parts of the service to meet the needs of the child.

Planning the Funeral Is a Family Process

In the planning of the funeral or memorial service it is useful to check in with each child to see if there is an age-appropriate role he or she would wish to serve in the service. A young child may place a flower on the casket, an older child may read a prayer, and a teenager may read a eulogy or choose a song to play on an instrument or as a recording. It is important to convey to the child that the invitation to participate in the service honors the child's importance but is not a requirement. Children should never be given the message that they must perform at the ceremony if they really loved the parent. Offering a few different choices is best. For example, children may help choose the prayers, flowers, or music and thus feel included without having to perform when they are acutely grieving.

Participation should be voluntary, not another overwhelming obligation or an experience that feels like being on display. It is important to give your child the message that love, grief, and coping are personal, and that the people who love your child want him or her to do what feels most personally helpful, not what others expect or demand. This includes permitting different children within the same family to make different choices about their roles in the ceremony.

"What Can We Do to Help?"

Often friends and family will want to be able to do something that is helpful. This is a wonderful time to ask friends to bring photos and write recollections about funny stories or special experiences they had with the parent who died. Sometimes when someone dies, it seems that no one is allowed to remember the imperfections or silly things the person did. Stories, lovingly told, that reflect a real person with real shortcomings present a parent who is an easier person for a child to remain connected to as he or she grows up. Children may be especially curious about memories others have of when the parent was a child, or stories that describe what the parent loved about being a parent or what the parent loved about his or her children. These stories and photos can be compiled into a book for the children to have access to now and in the future. (See Chapter 14 on leaving a legacy.)

Make Sure All Members of the Family Are Acknowledged

If you are the surviving parent or another relative of the parent who died, you will want to know the details of the memorial service in advance so you can prepare the child for what to expect. At times, when the organizers are outside the family, they may inadvertently be insensitive to the child's perspective. If photographs are shown, the children should be represented as equally as possible. Older children may want to have a say about which photographs of them are included. It is important that one child not feel ignored nor another feel embarrassed by a particular picture. If one child is acknowledged with flowers or asked to stand, then the others should be as well. This may seem obvious, but often it is overlooked and a child's feelings are unnecessarily hurt.

It is important that the surviving spouse not feel either marginalized or exposed by the photographs or stories that are shared. Sometimes, when the relationship between the parents has been conflicted, the friends and family of the parent who died will create a memorial service that essentially excludes the surviving parent. This can be painful for the surviving parent, can be confusing to the children, and can set the stage for the surviving parent to further disconnect from the circle of people important to the parent who died. The biggest losers in this scenario are the children, who then lose easy access to a community of people who knew and loved the parent who died.

Memorial Services

Memorial services need not occur in the difficult first days after a parent dies. Instead there can be time to plan something over weeks or months that captures aspects of the parent that can be celebrated by the community. Sometimes the family organizes a memorial service, and sometimes it grows in response to the parent's community, personal or professional, that wants to remember the person in this public way. When it is the community more than the family organizing this celebration, your child may choose to attend the event or choose not to do so. If a child chooses not to attend, you may want to videotape the event to allow your child the opportunity to view it at a later time of your child's choice. For those children who attend, it can be a wonderful opportunity to see that they are not grieving alone and to learn about their parent being appreciated in many ways and by many people.

Closing Words

Funerals and memorial services are religious, family, and community opportunities to remember and honor a loved one who has died. These are important events for children who have lost a parent. They remind children that others recognize how special and valued their parent was to many and provide another opportunity to say good-bye.

Surviving parents and other caretakers should seek as much detailed information about the events as possible before they take place. Preparing children for what they will see and what will happen is the best approach to diminishing feelings of being ignored or overwhelmed.

Parents may want to expose children to other end-of-life ceremonies associated with deaths in their extended family or in the community before a parent dies as a way of preparing their children for future losses. Attending these events is a good way to start a conversation about what was confusing, troubling, or reassuring about the ritual. Even the death of a loved pet can be a jumping-off point for discussing death, funerals, and how we remember those who are special to us. Death is an inevitable part of life. Including end-of-life ceremonies among a child's many experiences will help a child feel more comfortable and less afraid of this aspect of life.

Epilogue

Your Child's Bright Future

Good parenting helps pave the way for a child to have a bright future—a future that includes important relationships, hopefully one day a life partner, meaningful work, and satisfying leisure activities. This is a book about good parenting. It happens to focus on taking care of children when a parent is sick, but it mostly talks about things that would help any child grow up emotionally secure and healthy. The focus on understanding the impact of a parent's illness from a child's perspective guides the parenting strategies that will be best for your child. Many aspects of the book reflect the need for parents to have contingency plans for living with uncertainty. Parents with a known illness have additional pressure to do this planning, but we all live in an uncertain world and would do well to plan accordingly.

We hope the information on normal development and temperament has helped you understand your child's behavior and communications better. Attempting to understand the motivations that underlie the things a child says and the reasons for behavior is both important and complicated. It often feels more difficult to interpret actions or words when you have the added worry that you may be seeing signs of distress in response to your medical condition. Most often behavior and communications reflect a combination of a child's stage of development, temperament, and the specific ways the events in his life affect his routine—and your illness is simply one of many life events.

It would be odd if a child did not react to the changes imposed by a parent's illness. But as with other changes and challenges a child will face, a parent's illness need not knock a child off his or her developmental course. We have highlighted the importance of thinking about ways to keep a child's daily schedule consistent, protect child-centered family time, and improve communication from parent to child and child to parent. Knowing more about development and adjustment to a parent's illness often makes it easier to listen quietly and be attuned to your child's individual experience and perspective. Hopefully, you have a better road map now for keeping your child on track.

The chapters in this book offer different ways you can buffer your child from the most disruptive aspects of your medical illness. This includes focusing attention on the details of your child's life while allowing your child opportunities to talk openly with you about your illness, his or her specific worries, and the effect changes in you or in your family life have on your child. It also means having consistent rules and expectations that make family life go as smoothly as possible for everyone and utilizing a support network well. By recognizing common issues for children of sick parents, you can feel good about crafting an environment that more times than not can put your child's life in the center and your illness in the background.

A parent's illness teaches a child many life lessons. Be mindful that you will be the greatest influence in the lessons learned. You can teach your child to face challenges with strength, optimism, and humor. You can teach him or her to live every day to the fullest. Your child will learn how a family and community rally around someone who is ill, especially if the help you get is talked about openly and with appreciation. Your child can learn how people who love each other share difficult news in direct and respectful conversations.

Your child will discover that the same hard situation is hard in different ways for different family members and that those differences are best honored and not devalued. When facing challenges, it is normal for loving people to have a broad array of feelings, including being angry, disappointed, and frustrated at times. Challenges such as the impact of your medical condition are an opportunity for your child to explore and expand coping skills. You can help your child to do that while feeling safe. As much as you might wish to remove your illness from your child's life experience and your family's, you can't. But you can make it a growth experience.

Some parents will have read this book with the worry that they or their coparent face the possibility or reality of an untimely death. It is a painful prospect to contemplate your child continuing to grow up without you or without the active participation of his or her other parent. While this is a major loss for your child and for you, it is important to make the most of the time you have together and to leave your child the best possible legacy of love, hope, and consideration. An important aspect of this is imparting your confidence that your child will go on to live a happy and productive life, while carrying the loved deceased parent in his or her heart.

We have spoken with many parents who themselves had a parent die in childhood. They have provided wonderful insights into what helped them. They remind us of the importance of offering children opportunities for communication during the difficult times before and after a parent's death, and the value of talking calmly and lovingly about the parent who died, or working through old conflicts or hurts. These adults also provide the most compelling demonstration of how strong, successful, and fulfilled an adult who lost a parent in childhood can be. We have heard many examples from children and adults about the ways in which facing and living through the enormous challenge of a parent's death made them feel more capable of facing all the lesser challenges in their lives. As one happily married mother told me, "After my father died when I was eight, with any new challenge I would just tell myself—how hard can this be? It isn't like Dad dying. I think it made me a little bit fearless." Today she is a practicing surgeon.

We hope that this book has been interesting, useful, and comforting. We share a love of children, admiration for the incredible efforts of parents, a recognition of how challenging parenting is, a respect for the diversity in loving families, and a deep belief in the resiliency of children and in the strength that resides in family, friends, and community. We hope we have communicated that in this book.

Your feedback is more than welcome. We especially appreciate hearing from parents who have discovered helpful approaches through their family's experiences with an illness that they would like to share with others. You can contact us at the Department of Child Psychiatry, YAW 6A, Massachusetts General Hospital, 15 Parkman Street, Boston, MA 02114. We feel privileged to have come to know the vibrant community of sick parents with healthy families. We wish you and your family well.

Resources

Disease-Specific Organizations

For more information on your specific illness, call or visit the website of the association, foundation, or organization that represents people with your medical condition. A few are listed below. Many more can be found by typing the name of your illness into an Internet search engine.

ALS Association
alsa.org

American Cancer Society
cancer.org

American Diabetes Association
diabetes.org

American Heart Association
americanheart.org

Brain Injury Association of America
biausa.org

Colitis Foundation
colitisfoundation.com

Cystic Fibrosis Foundation
cff.org

Epilepsy Foundation
epilepsyfoundation.org

HIV/AIDS
managinghiv.com

National Multiple Sclerosis Society
nmss.org

National Neurofibromatosis Foundation
nf.org

Pulmonary Fibrosis Foundation
pulmonaryfibrosis.org

Financial and Legal Information

Social Security
socialsecurity.gov

Provides information on Social Security programs and allows you to apply for disability benefits online.

Government Benefits
lsc.gov

Listing of legal aid organizations offering free legal services for individuals who cannot afford legal fees.

Children's Mental Health

American Academy of Child and Adolescent Psychiatry
aacap.org

American Academy of Pediatrics
aap.org

Additional Resources

Conversations from the Heart: Resources for Talking with Children About a Parent's Serious Illness

This is a comprehensive list of books, articles, websites, videos, and community support groups compiled by J. D. Perloff and V. M. Rizzo. It is available for download at thelifeinstitute.org.

Books

It is beyond the scope of this book to list a full bibliography of books that you and your family might find useful. These are a few of our favorites. Consult your local librarian or bookshop staff member or check a Web-based bookseller for additional resources.

DePaola, T. *Nana Upstairs and Nana Downstairs*. New York: Puffin Books, 1973. A storybook about death.

Faber, A., and E. Mazlish. *How to Talk So Kids Will Listen and Listen So Kids Will Talk*. New York: Harper Resources, 1999.

Fitzgerald, H. *The Grieving Teen: A Guide for Teenagers and Their Friends*. New York: Fireside Books, 2000.

Gardner, D., and T. Gardner. "When Life Happens." *The Motley Fool Personal Finance Workbook*. New York: Simon and Schuster, 2003.

Harpham, W. T. *When a Parent Has Cancer: A Guide to Caring for Your Children*. New York: Perennial Currents, 2004.

Kalb, R. C., ed. *Multiple Sclerosis: A Guide for Families*. New York: Demos Medical Publishing, 1998.

Krementz, J. *How It Feels When a Parent Dies*. New York: Knopf, 1981.

Mayes, L. C., and D. J. Cohen. *The Yale Child Study Center Guide to Understanding Your Child: Healthy Development from Birth to Adolescence*. Boston: Little, Brown and Co., 2003.

Rapaport, W. S. *When Diabetes Hits Home*. Alexandria, VA: American Diabetes Association, 1998.

Shuman, R., and J. Schwartz. *Living with Multiple Sclerosis: A Handbook for Families*. New York: Collier Books, 1994.

Turecki, S., and L. Tonner. *The Difficult Child*. (Revised edition.) New York: Bantam Publishing, 2000.

Viorst, J. *The Tenth Good Thing About Barney*. New York: Aladdin Paperbacks, 1988. A storybook about death.

Watnik, W. *Child Custody Made Simple: Understanding the Laws of Child Custody and Support*. Claremont, CA: Single Parent Press, 2003.

Index

About the Authors

Paula K. Rauch, M.D., is the founding director of the Massachusetts General Hospital (MGH) Cancer Center parenting program: Parenting at a Challenging Time (PACT) and director of the Child Psychiatry Consultation Service to Pediatrics at MGH, where she has practiced child psychiatry for twenty years. A graduate of Amherst College and the University of Cincinnati College of Medicine, she is an assistant professor of psychiatry at Harvard Medical School. Dr. Rauch has devoted her professional career to helping children cope with family illness. Dr. Rauch was honored with the 2003 Compassionate Caregiver Award by the Kenneth B. Schwartz Center. She and her husband have three children.

Anna (Nina) Muriel, M.D., M.P.H., is a staff child psychiatrist in the PACT parenting program at Massachusetts General Hospital. She also works in the Child Psychiatry Consultation Service to Pediatrics at MGH and in private practice. A graduate of Brown University and Tufts University School of Medicine, she is currently an instructor in psychiatry at Harvard Medical School. She enjoys teaching and has interest in the public health aspects of parental illness and its effect on families and children. Raised in New York City, she now lives in the Boston area with her family.